The God Who Walks Slowly

The God Who Walks Slowly

*Reflections on Mission with
Kosuke Koyama*

Benjamin Aldous

scm press

© Benjamin Aldous 2022
Published in 2022 by SCM Press
Editorial office
3rd Floor, Invicta House,
108–114 Golden Lane,
London EC1Y OTG, UK

www.scmpress.co.uk

SCM Press is an imprint of Hymns Ancient & Modern Ltd
(a registered charity)

Hymns Ancient & Modern® is a registered trademark of
Hymns Ancient & Modern Ltd
13A Hellesdon Park Road, Norwich,
Norfolk NR6 5DR, UK

British Library Cataloguing in Publication data
A catalogue record for this book is available
from the British Library

978-0-334-06111-3

Typeset by Regent Typesetting
Printed and bound by
CPI Group (UK) Ltd

Contents

Preface   vii

1 Introduction   1
2 Walking: The Importance of Slowing Down   30
3 Seeing: Notes in the Margins   65
4 Talking: Shut Up and Listen, Will You!   95
5 Surrendering: Nailed Down!   126
6 Conclusion: In Him All Things Hold Together   155

Bibliography   170
Index of Names and Subjects   174

Preface

This book is, in part, the product of cultural discombobulation. When I returned to the UK in early 2019 after 15 years in Cambodia and South Africa I was profoundly aware that coming back was not necessarily 'coming home'. Crossing boundaries, making home in other parts of the world for extended periods, is a common occurrence for more and more people. In fact, it might be one of the defining traits of the twentieth and twenty-first centuries. Some of us have chosen or felt called to these relocations. Others have been forced to cross borders through no fault of their own. Whatever the particular conditions, writing about these experiences can be liberating. The critical theorist Theodore Adorno wrote, 'for a man who no longer has homeland writing becomes a place to live'. Writing this book with Koyama as my friend and guide has been about reflecting on my own experiences through his lenses and bringing them into dialogue with the UK context. Writing has helped me, to some extent, 'land'.

Discovering the work of Kosuke Koyama was like finding a fellow pilgrim who seemed to reflect back to me the dangerous ideals of power, speed and the desire to be spectacular. These are problems that the Church tends towards at times. Koyama was a gift to me when much of my ministry had taken place among the powerless, the slow and the lowly – in short, those clinging on to life.

This book, then, is the product of 15 years of life and work outside the UK and I am thankful to those who I have had the enormous privilege of working alongside, particularly in Cambodia and South Africa. My life has been overwhelmingly shaped by the opportunity to work with colleagues in churches and communities in Phnom Penh, Neak Loeung, Durban and Cape Town. I'm thankful to Hak Hyun and Soeung Won, Nobue, Srey Mom, Vachana, Catherine, Ali and Juliet, Vicky and Bruce, Matt and Sean, Etienne and Beth, Keegan and Lindsay, Auntie Rae, Dean and Miché, and others in those locations.

I'm also thankful to my wife Sharon and my children Talia, Amelie, Reuben and Esther, who have been constant companions and friends in the writing process, and especially Sharon for the lino cut she made which became the cover of the book you are now holding. I am grateful to Peter Houston, Al Barrett, Steve Hollinghurst and others who made helpful comments on early drafts of chapters and made insightful observations about flow and structure. Any inadequacies in the final text are my own.

Parts of these chapters often started life as blog posts (musings of the jazzgoat https://thejazzgoat.wordpress.com) and versions of some chapters appeared in various guises at workshops and conferences. I am thankful to all those who commented, gave helpful suggestions and were generally encouraging, including members of the Mission Research Network and staff and students at the Queens Foundation in Birmingham, where I am an honorary research fellow. Various versions of Chapter 2 appeared at a workshop at Queens, Birmingham and in Kampen, the Netherlands. I'm also thankful to the staff team at Churches Together in England (CTE), especially General Secretary Paul Goodliff who gave me specific weeks to write during my work, and Bishop Mike Royal for his enthusiasm.

Benjamin Aldous
Pentecost 2022

I

Introduction

Like many children who can remember back to the days of the BBC's *Record Breakers*, presented by trumpeter Roy Castle and the mega-brained Norris McWhirter, I remain fascinated by the *Guinness Book of Records*. I still have the 1989 edition which was a Christmas present when I was 13. It contains a collection of records of human endeavour and oddness. Perhaps, like others, I have been particularly interested in records concerning the fastest, the heaviest, the loudest, the biggest, the longest. For example, the curious pictures of Robert Wadlow, the tallest man in the world at 2 metres 72 centimetres according to irrefutable evidence, always fascinated me, probably on account of me being the smallest boy in my class. Or the longest moustache in the world belonging to Ram Singh Chauhan at an unfathomable 4 metres 29 centimetres.

Apart from the sloth, which is recorded as the slowest-moving mammal in the 1989 edition, there are almost no other celebrations of being slow. Being the slowest at something is not celebrated in most cultures. But this book is rooted in the idea of slowness; of a God who is slow, who slows us down and invites us to live in a more '*time*full' way.

The 'turn' towards slowness in the frantic, hectic modern world is well embodied in the story of Carlo Petrini, who is the founder of the slow food movement. This movement was, in part, a protest against McDonald's who were trying to open a restaurant on the Spanish Steps in Rome in the mid-1980s. The slow food movement stands as an alternative to fast food. It takes seriously regionality, locality and time – lots of it – in order to eat a good nourishing meal. As a result, we are seeing a resurgence in artisan processes, from brewing beer, distilling whisky, exploring ancient rituals for making cheese; the list goes on.

My guess is that we have all had moments in our lives when we have just wanted to get off the treadmill that is life. I wonder if that has been an ever-increasing problem from the advent of the industrial revolution when human beings' daily rhythms were increasingly mechanized. This is in contrast to an agrarian society which revolves around seasonal, communal and intense work patterns at planting and harvest followed by the patient work of waiting and watching. In an industrial society, human worth is reduced to factors of production which results in the loss of cyclical and seasonal time. An industrial society feeds the beast of factories, nourishing the machines that never sleep. This shift has been a turning point in human history.

Subsequently, the world is exhausted because it has been going too fast. People have been living beyond their natural capacities for too long. Our world is time squeezed, condensing lives and livelihoods into shorter and shorter timescales. We watch global events unfold in real time from multiple angles, often on our smartphones, while slumped on the couch. Our expectations of how quickly events should unfold are shaped by these contractions in time and perceptions of how fast we can go. This ranges from my mild irritation that my emails are not receiving the instant replies I think they deserve to the time it takes for a dictator to be removed from power as the population take to the streets, mobilized via WhatsApp and Facebook messenger.

Our inability to live timefully spills over into our ministry and mission. This is fuelled by an existential anxiety about the Church in the future and fearing that our place in the world may be less significant than we'd like. We have often been caught up in survival mode. That was at times my experience leading a congregation in Cape Town. I felt as if I was spending the vast majority of my time making Sunday happen, and when people dropped out or didn't turn up I'd fill the gap. Jump on the guitar, do the notices, be the service leader, all making me feel tired and resentful. It's a story I'm sure many reading this book will be familiar with. We are drawn into the narrative that 'to be busy is to be important', a signal of how much we are doing and how much we are needed. We are suspicious of those who have the capacity to waste time with others, who aren't hardwired into the Protestant work ethic. The answer seems to be – obviously – to stop and then slow down to walking pace.

As mentioned in the Preface, much of my own theological journey is rooted in 15 years of living and working in Cambodia and South Africa. From late 2004 until 2010 I lived in Cambodia, a nation largely overlooked in the flow of world history, a pawn in the games between world powers. For those five years I worked mostly alongside young Cambodian leaders who were often only a few years younger than me. I knew right from the outset I had little to offer. I could bring my creativity, my presence, a little bit of theological education, but mostly it was empty hands.

The most joy-filled memories during those years were my weekly visits to a small village. Every week on Sunday afternoon, I rode my faithful Suzuki 150 up national road 11. Usually, I had Sokha and Vachana on the back laughing, joking, teasing me about my poor barang[1] driving. We would turn off right towards Batti village. It was a bumpy road, sometimes impossible to drive along during the rainy season. Although I had been learning Khmer, the national Cambodian language, for four years, being able to truly communicate was still a struggle. Each week we would spend the initial part of our time surrounded by children, sometimes up to 90 of them, playing games, teaching songs, talking, laughing, goofing around. Afterwards we would climb into one of the typical Cambodian houses on stilts (with pigs and chickens below) and have a little service with the only Christian family in the whole village. Om and his wife were faithful believers. Their teenage children were sweet, alert and concerned for their mother who was terribly thin and often very sick. Occasionally I would share a short homily. My linguistic imbecility was obvious to anyone who listened. It took much concentration and effort to craft my homily. Often, I was saying the right words but people had given up listening, given up trying to decipher what I was attempting to say through my mangled Khmer. But there were moments when it seems that my verbal inadequacies were translated somehow by the Spirit and miraculously broke into my listeners' hearts. The words of Dorothy Day sum it up really: 'What we do is very little. Christ took that little and increased it. What we do is so little that we may seem to be constantly failing. He met with apparent failure on the Cross. But unless the seeds fall into the earth and die, there is no harvest.'[2]

My work over those five years was very little and most often very slow.

In South Africa, I helped in wealthy, white churches in suburbs of Durban and led a multi-racial congregation in Cape Town. In Cape Town, I had a congregation made up of South Africans who were still working out how to live with one another more fully. Many of the older members were men and women who had suffered the utter indignity of being forcibly removed from their homes and sent off to the Cape Flats through the apartheid government's Group Areas Act. As I sat and drank tea on home visits, I would almost always hear the pain of those days bubble up. Pain that would never be completely subdued – the pain of walking past the house your parents once owned but was now declared a 'whites only' area and the acute injustice of being unable to return. The pain of a colleague in the teaching profession who had become politically active and died in police custody. South Africa is littered with these stories. The congregation was also home to others from sub-Saharan Africa, many of whom had navigated the creases of the continent, sometimes taking many years to reach the relative safety of Cape Town. They brought their own stories of loss, sometimes unimaginable in brutality. Added to this, we had a dynamic – and at times chaotic – children's ministry with many unaccompanied children coming to our family service each week from the military base next door (the church was originally a garrison church built for the British

4

military in 1834). Very often I was at a loss to know quite how to help a congregation navigate its way into abundant life with so many people from different places with deep wounds and many needs, yet those years in Cape Town were some of the most wonderful and profoundly challenging. In these spaces I saw that many treading the path as Jesus' followers were struggling. It taught me to ask questions about power, status and about whose voices were really being heard and amplified.

When I returned to the UK in December 2018, and prior to starting work for Churches Together in England (CTE),[3] I had a few months to prepare for my new role. I was asked to preach in a local church with a handful of people in the congregation who teach theology at university level. I quoted a few lines from Kosuke Koyama at the end of my sermon. Afterwards, one of the university lecturers came to ask me about Koyama and admitted she had never heard of him. It made me realize that perhaps Koyama should be better known, given the important role he has played in ecumenical and contextual theologies. In fact, I ended up reading an anthology of key texts and voices from the twentieth-century ecumenical movement. Koyama's speech to the Melbourne 1980 World Conference on Mission and Evangelism seemed so prophetic for our own time 40 years later.[4]

I have found Koyama a delight to read. Writing in a second language makes his prose inventive, quirky and refreshing since he doesn't rely on idiomatic English language expressions or devices. I don't often laugh out loud when reading theology, but he has made me do that at times – whether it's with a chapter of his book called 'The Face With Eyebrows Shaved Off!' or his suspicions about how Xerox machines really work. His ability to mix and interrelate old and new images of world cultures is the heart of Koyama's genius as a teacher.[5]

A few caveats are necessary for you as a reader of this book. First, this is *not* a systematic introduction to the work of Koyama, although I do hope that by reading this book you will want to explore his writings for yourself and get an idea of his main themes.[6] (I have a secret hope that you'll become interested in seeking out theological voices from other corners of the world too.) I use Koyama as a conversation partner in each chapter, drawing on what I consider to be some of his most important themes throughout his career. I hope that there is a sort of *prophetic dialogue*,[7] or perhaps trialogue, between Koyama's theological reflections on mission and ministry, the current UK landscape, and my own journey.

Second, what follows is not a comprehensive review of Koyama's work. I draw on a wide range of his writing and attempt to deal with his core ideas, but there are things that I've not been able to write about. For instance, I don't touch on Koyama's treatment of Buddhism and his extensive writing on approaching other religious traditions, for which he is well known. Nor do I consider myself to be an expert on Koyama. When I told a friend that I was writing a book for SCM Press, she said, 'Are you going to be the world's leading expert on Koyama?' I made a face in reply. Like any sane person, I reject the notion of being the world's leading expert on anything. This book is simply a small, humble offering into the world of Koyama scholarship and mission.

Third, in the process of publishing this book, my faithful editor insisted I make the flow of the book more logical, to have more of an internal flow, and for it to be longer than I had originally intended (usually, writers are asked to cull their writings!). It's somewhat ironic that this was the kind of criticism levelled at Koyama himself. Part of me wanted to write 50 chapters of three pages each in the vein of Koyama, which I have found to be a more natural response to the way I write and often think – basically in blog musings. I think Victoria Erickson had a point when she wrote a chapter for a Koyama *Festschrift* and said, 'in the great Koyama tradition we will make it up as we go along'.[8]

Fourth, much theological writing is autobiographical, and what follows in these pages does not depart from that basic assumption. Koyama has been important for me. He helped me to *begin* to do theology in an Asian context. For five years, as I lived and worked in Cambodia, the imagery of water buffalo, green mangoes, sticky rice, the Mekong river and the general slowness of life in rural South East Asian contexts made sense to me, because of Koyama. He was a man who was committed to 'theology from below'. His theological thinking gave priority to farmers over Thomas Aquinas and Karl Barth.[9] Looking back, I didn't take Koyama seriously enough. I only skim-read *Waterbuffalo Theology*. Although I was trying to live out what it means to do contextual theology, much of my evangelical heritage made me suspicious of Koyama. I look back on certain aspects of my time living in Cambodia and South Africa with dismay. Dismay that I could and should have done things differently. I could have been slower. I should have been a much better listener and learner.

Finally, in true Koyama style, I hope this book offers more questions than it does concrete answers to particular mission challenges in twenty-first-century Britain. In later chapters, I have probably posed more questions than given anything like concrete answers. In the post-pandemic era that seems a reasonable thing to do, given so many of us are reappraising our lives and those of our churches.

A biographical sketch

Kosuke Koyama was born on 10 December 1929 in Tokyo, and in many ways was a rarity in Japanese culture. He was born into a Christian family, his paternal grandfather having come to faith in the 1860s. His grandfather encouraged the family to read the Bible, although Koyama admits he found the names of Peter, Paul, Moses and Elijah curious to pronounce. The grandchildren were encouraged to share their ideas of what the stories meant to them. Koyama felt that because of this, the Bible was always a companion book that initiated fascinating and serious discussions about our lives in the world. He wrote just after his retirement in 1997, 'I hold today that the Bible is the Word of God not because it is so defined by the church, but because it speaks to us urgently and deeply.'[10] It's easy to see how that early encouragement from his grandfather became part of Koyama's own starting point for doing and writing theology. Perhaps his three most vital books – *No Handle on the Cross*, *Three Mile an Hour God* and *50 Meditations* – are essentially shorter musings or reflections of two or three pages, often rooted in a particular passage or story from Scripture.

There was another text that Koyama encountered as a ten-year-old. *Pilgrim's Progress*, although beyond his comprehension at the time, made a deep impact on him:

> I can see that the book introduced me to the Christian understanding of history. Our lives, and even the great panorama of human history, have beginnings and ends that contain the movement (i.e., the pilgrim's progress) toward God. This understanding of life and of history gives a fundamental orientation for the Christian understanding of mission.[11]

Many of the major themes in Koyama's writing were developed in the early part of his life and out of the deeply traumatic experience of living in Tokyo in his teenage years during World War Two. He writes that 'between 1941 and 1945 I experienced utter confusion, violence, and destruction. Night after night the bombs rained down upon us. Yet, somehow, the idea that our life, personally and collectively, must be a movement toward God survived in my soul.'[12] Later, in his thirties, the recurring themes of slowness and inefficiency were born out of his direct experience of learning the Thai language and working with the farming community near Chiang Mai. On reflection, Koyama said that 'being unable to produce certain sounds, my tongue was twisted, my lungs pained, and my intelligence humiliated. Learning the Thai language was my second spiritual baptism, a baptism into the unfamiliar sounds and symbols of a different culture and religion.'[13]

He also developed other important themes around anti-imperialism and anti-idolatry[14] as he saw his own nation of Japan damaged by the cult of the emperor. In ecumenical circles he spoke consistently about the need for ecumenical theology to find its life and hope in the idea of Christ at the periphery.[15] He took a gentle, non-aggressive approach to other faiths, seeing beauty and truth in them yet holding on securely to the centrality of Jesus Christ. In short, although he wrote 40 years ago, his words continue to have a prophetic edge. Koyama's theological method and his missiology can be a refreshment and challenge to the patterns and rhythms of mission being explored today.

In the remainder of this chapter, I explore how Koyama can be seen as a contextual theologian. I will explain the global historical context in which he operated and wrote; and outline how Koyama was a Japanese theologian who, although he lived outside Asia for a good part of his life, was shaped by Japanese thinking. I will also consider how, as a 'pan Christian', Koyama straddled the sometimes painful and fractured divide between ecumenical and evangelical worlds without any real intention of doing so.

Koyama and contextual theology

Koyama was always considering micro and macro context in his writing – whether his meditations find their starting point in a towering pine tree on his morning walk in New Zealand ('I touched this morning the same spot of this great tree and I feel assured'),[16] or reflecting on the damage the cult of the emperor caused the entire nation of Japan. In whatever way we want to position Koyama, one thing is certain: he was a theologian who took context seriously.

The Catholic missiologist Stephen Bevans has famously said that all theology is contextual theology. Any serious missiological work takes context seriously. The story of the gospel is a story of particularity, of concrete everydayness. The gospel is never disembodied. Jesus is the son of Nazareth, born in the Jewish backwaters of the vast Roman empire in first-century Palestine. The word made flesh revels in situatedness. The story of the gospel is recast in a myriad of human situations.

Contextual theology is a theological 'turn to the subjective', which has been a cause for alarm for those who have always begun with a text. Human contexts are made up of our families, neighbourhoods, villages, towns, cities, nations, past, present and inevitably future in a complex, dynamic way – always in some kind of flux. While these are always 'local' they have increasingly been impinged upon by global factors. Just as local has been influenced by the global, it might be better to think about different modes of situatedness.

The rise of conscious approaches to context came about most notably in the 1960s with the liberation theology from Gutiérrez, Boff, Segundo and others in South America. Soon there were other contextual theologies born out of the experiences of suffering and marginalization in its many forms, leading to feminist theology, black theology, queer theology, Hispanic theology, etc. The term 'contextual theology', however, formally came to prominence through the Fund for Theological Education in 1972 and has since been developed in multiple directions. Perhaps, though, the most prominent of those writing on contextual theology is Stephen Bevans himself. For the sake of space, I'm using Bevans as the main interlocuter and drawing on his influential book *Models*, which he first sketched out as far back as 1985[17] but developed more fully in 1992.

Bevans says that contextual theology is a way of theologizing that takes seriously the *experience of the past*, recorded in the Scriptures and preserved and defended in the churches' traditions, in mutual dialogue with *experiences of the present*. But context not only shapes the content and method of our theologizing. It also determines the questions we ask and highlights the things we see as important.[18]

In *Models*, Bevans suggests that one issue in contextual theology is that it can be done out of one of two predominant centres: a creation-centred approach, or a redemption-centred perspective.[19] The creation-centred approach sees the world and creation as sacramental or, to put it another way, 'human experience and so context is generally good'.[20] God reveals

Godself in the wild ragged terrain of the world. This calls us to take seriously the world outside the altar and the sanctuary and acknowledge how God is at work in the sacred ordinariness of life. The redemption-centred perspective, says Bevans, 'is characterized by the conviction that culture and human experience are either in need of a radical transformation or in need of total replacement'.[21] Out of these two centres Bevans suggests six models, though he would be the first to admit that models are inherently limited. For example, if I go and look around a new housing estate and see the scale model of the site in the developer's office, I get an idea of how it's going to be laid out, the general scale and topography of the place, but I can't inhabit it or put my body in it. Bevans says that, 'it is of utmost importance to understand that models are constructions'. No model can account for all the data of a particular area or for the complexity of a theological position or doctrine, but they are helpful for navigating our way around the world ... if we treat them in the right way.

Bevans's six models are initially best understood by seeing them visually mapped out in the diagram below which comes from his book *Models of Contextual Theology*. These models are *Translation, Anthropological, Praxis, Synthetic, Transcendental* and *Countercultural*:

A map of the models of contextural theology

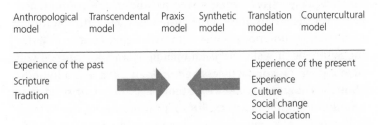

| Anthropological model | Transcendental model | Praxis model | Synthetic model | Translation model | Countercultural model |

Experience of the past
Scripture
Tradition

Experience of the present
Experience
Culture
Social change
Social location

Diagram taken from S. B. Bevans, 2002, *Models of Contextual Thology*, Maryknoll, NY: Orbis Books, p. 32, used with permission.

The Translation and Countercultural models sit at the right-hand side of the map rooted as they are in the experiences of the past witnessed in Scripture and tradition. Those proponents of the Translation model would argue that this is 'possibly the oldest way to take the context of theologizing seriously'.[22] The Translation model is emphatic about the message of the gospel as an unchanging message. There is a kernel of gospel with a contextualizing husk.

At the other end of the continuum is the Anthropological model. Bevans says that the 'model centres on the value and goodness of Anthropos, the human person. It is within every person, and every society and social location and every culture, that God manifests the divine presence.'[23] In essence, the Anthropological model hinges on the idea that human nature – and therefore human context – is good, holy and valuable. One of the weaknesses of this model is that it can fall into the trap of being overly romantic about human nature and culture.

Somewhere in the centre of the continuum sits the Synthetic model. This model is 'both/and': 'It takes pains to keep the integrity of the traditional message whilst acknowledging the importance of taking all the aspects of context seriously.'[24] But it's important to understand, as Bevans points out, that 'synthetic' doesn't mean artificial. Synthetic means a synthesis of the previous models, straddling the sometimes diametrically opposed creation-centred approach with the redemption-centred perspective. Sitting in the middle of the continuum it preserves the importance of the gospel message with traditional doctrinal formulations while acknowledging context. Within the Synthetic model there is an openness, an ambiguity, a way of living with incompleteness and dialogue. There is a humility about learning from others – be they part of the Christian community, or another faith tradition, or none.

For Bevans, Koyama is an example of the Synthetic model at work. Bevans says, 'I find a strong dialectic in much of what he writes between high sensitivity to cultural reality on the one hand and a strong sense of truth of the gospel message on the other.'[25] Koyama very often roots his missiological reflections in biblical passages but refuses to be coerced into only traditional Western-influenced readings of a text. This is born also out of the experience of the rice paddies in northern Thailand. An example of this is his creative playfulness when explaining how Thai Christians season their faith with Aristotelian pepper and Buddhist salt.[26] On his ministry in Thailand, Koyama reflected on 'how Western – is the Christian vocabulary to the ears of my Thai neighbours'. He began to see how Thai Christians flavoured terms like *sin*, *incarnation* and *redemption through his blood* with Buddhist salt since Theravada Buddhism permeates so much of Thai culture, existence and modes of thought. There should not be a collapse of these terms into purely Buddhist concepts as this leads to syncretism. Koyama says, 'Our dilemma is this: if we say, "salvation through the blood of Jesus", our Thai audience is completely lost.'[27] There has to be a dialogical relationship between the gospel as it is transmitted in its often Western guise with the host culture.

Another kind of Synthetic model approach can be seen in Koyama's insistence that the finger of God does not work comprehensively. Attempting to dissolve what he calls 'divine beauty contests of – my religion is better than yours',[28] Koyama says that 'a comprehensive God is an obvious God. The "obvious" God is an idol. Idols we can tame, but we cannot domesticate the living God.'[29] Koyama reminds us that God is not found as a passive answer but an initiator of relationship; God refuses to be experienced as a series of theological factoids. Koyama says that in Japanese culture to say 'Jesus is the answer' is banal (but perhaps our banal culture notices it less?). It sounds awkward, cheap and superficial and would be understood as saying that Christianity works mechanically, therefore it has no significant spiritual dimension.[30] To inhabit the Synthetic model is to live with paradox and incompleteness, to find creative ways to work out a dialogue between text and context.

Koyama was always able to hold in tension his love for Scripture with his honouring of culture. Maybe this is rooted in his own experience of the conversations with his grandfather who, Koyama says, 'was impressed by this man who was able to say

Jesus is Lord without ever making derogatory comments about Japanese culture of Buddhism'.[31]

Finally, perhaps there is an inherent synthetic approach found in other Japanese Christians. The stencil-cut artist Sadao Watanabe, who was a little older than Koyama, produced a huge body of work mostly based on biblical texts. John Kohan writes that, early in his Christian discipleship, Watanabe was 'browsing the shelves in a Christian bookstore one day and was struck by the fact that almost all the covers were illustrated with pictures of European religious paintings and sculptures. There was nothing that spoke to the Japanese in their own visual language.'[32] His artistic journey over the next 60 years changed that fundamentally, creating work that fused the text of Scripture with the context of *mingei* folk art and ordinary Japanese people. Kohan again says, 'any westerner with the vaguest knowledge of the Bible will recognize as the story of Noah's Ark looks to Japanese viewers more like a huge cricket cage filled with rats, tigers, oxen, hare, monkeys, and other animal signs of the zodiac'.[33]

Koyama and the global historical context

No one lives in a historical vacuum. While Koyama was shaped by his early experiences in Japan and his time in Thailand, Singapore, New Zealand and finally in the USA, he wrote into a global historical context. Koyama's most important writing took place between the early 1970s into the late 1980s although he continued to teach and write into the mid-2000s. He wrote in the context of the crisis and flamboyance of the 1970s and 1980s.

The twentieth century embodies some of humanity's greatest achievements and its most horrific atrocities. It has been shaped by two devastating world wars and the continued rancour of the Cold War juxtaposed with enormous bounds in scientific and technological advance. Like many of his generation, Koyama was utterly shaped by World War Two. He continued throughout his life to return to what he had witnessed and experienced first-hand in Tokyo. He was an outspoken critic of the nuclear arms race, and the rise in the use of – and dependence on – technology. He was suspicious of this power and speed, and much of what Koyama wrote about was, I'm sure, a response to the unfolding challenges of modern life that he witnessed.

The 1970s saw the end of the post-World War Two economic boom with many Western nations moving into recession. *The Limits to Growth* report published by the Club of Rome in 1972, based on five variables of population, food production, industrialization, pollution and the consumption of non-renewable resources, revealed the grave trajectory the world was on. This was exacerbated by the oil crisis in 1974. The 1970s were punctuated by political scandals (most notably Watergate) and continued conflicts, with a troublesome second Indo China war resulting in genocide in Cambodia, and the USA looking foolish in Vietnam. These were mostly framed in Cold War binary terms.

This was certainly true of the considerable violence in Mozambique and Angola and other communist-backed national and liberationist movements in Africa, East Asia and South America. South Africa was beginning to boil over with the Soweto uprising sparked by the death of Steve Biko. Towards the end of the decade the Iranian revolution of 1979 saw the overthrow of the Shah and the installation of an Islamic theocracy led by Ayatollah Khomeini. Technologically, the 1970s saw the launch of the Apple II computer in 1977 and the beginnings of a home-computer revolution that is still unfolding at pace. The year before, Concorde's inaugural flight meant it was possible to have breakfast in London and be in New York for lunch. The Shinkansen train running from Tokyo to Osaka had already carried a billion passengers by 1976.

The 1980s continued to bear witness to the development of technology. In 1980, CNN was launched as the first 24-hour news channel. The following year came MTV. Fractures in the communist bloc began to appear – perhaps most clearly visible in Gorbachev's appointment by the Politburo as leader of the Soviet Union. Gen Xers like myself may recall these days well. I can vividly remember watching the Tiananmen Square uprising on TV on 5 June 1989 and the death of Tank Man. A few months later, I watched – fascinated – the pulling down and eventual collapse of the Berlin Wall in November. The Wall as a symbol of the crumbling of communist power against the seemingly unfettered growth of capitalism was acute. As Gen Xers with our Commodore 64s and ZX Spectrums, we were the first generation to attempt home computing and to watch as cassette tapes loaded up our video games. The crazy growth of the 1980s was fuelled by the rapid development in the advancement of technology.

But our relationship with technology was changing dramatically and expectations about how that relationship could bring human beings fulfilment were somewhat utopian. I explore some of Koyama's prophetic words around technology and 'efficiency' in Chapter 5. As Koyama liked to say, 'Jesus Christ dislikes speedism and sensationalism.'[34]

Koyama in the Japanese context[35]

It is important to acknowledge that while Koyama's early experiences of life in Japan, especially during the war, shaped his theological perspective, he spent a large part of his life outside his native Japan. He left Japan in 1952, almost penniless except for a one-way ticket to study theology at Drew University in New Jersey. After being awarded his PhD from Princeton in 1959 he went to Thailand in 1960 and subsequently held academic posts in Singapore, Dunedin in New Zealand, and finally at Union Theological Seminary in New York. Koyama never returned to live in Japan in any extended way. While he was shaped by his Japanese heritage and inheritance, his 'later theological development was largely independent from the currents of theology in Japan'.[36] Despite this, Koyama's theology is shaped by his Japanese cultural Christian heritage. Some of his themes around suffering and self-denial are important to the experience and theology of other Japanese theologians and reflect the influence of indigenous cultural attitudes stemming from Japanese history, particularly Bushido.[37]

Koyama was often critical of his homeland. He returned again and again to the issue of the emperor and the idolatry he saw. The third part of his book *Three Mile an Hour God* is entitled 'Nation Searching'[38] and contains a number of personal reflections on Koyama's wrestling and wrangling with his own nation's past and its path for the future.

The Japanese continue to be one of the largest unreached people groups in the world. Is this in part because of Japan's isolation from the West for close to 250 years? Or the inability of the early Jesuits and later American Protestants to synthesize the faith? Or perhaps the cultural homogeneity of the Japanese nation is impenetrable in any depth to many who attempt to make their home among Japanese people?

Christianity came to Japan in the mid-sixteenth century, initially with Portuguese traders and shortly after with the Jesuit leader Francis Xavier. In the absence of a central government, the Jesuits were to have a virtual monopoly of the island for close to a century. Xavier engaged Buddhist monks in dialogue, some of whom were baptized. Others from the noble classes – who perhaps saw baptism as a way of securing trade with the Portuguese – followed suit. Koyama thought that Xavier and the Jesuits in general had taken Japanese culture seriously, noting that what impressed Japanese people most was that they placed equal importance on the funerals of both rich and poor, treating them fairly.[39] On the one hand, Xavier brought to the Japanese the story of the supreme value and dignity of each human being in the eyes of God, but on the other saw the Japanese largely as pagans and idolaters, enemies of God under the power of the devil.[40] This period from 1549 until 1650 is often dubbed the 'Christian Century'.

Towards the end of the 1500s there was growing persecution. The westernization of Christian converts and the suspicion towards Christians from Hideyoshi – as well as political tensions between Spanish and Portuguese missionaries – saw a growing number of martyrs. The crucifixion of 26 Franciscans and Jesuits (the majority of whom were Japanese) just outside Nagasaki on 5 February 1597 continues to be significant in the history of the Church in Japan. Shusaku Edo's *Silence* narrates some of the stories well. For the next 250 years the nation was effectively closed while a remnant of hidden Christians kept faith alive.

It wasn't until the 1850s that Japan was opened up again. Under Emperor Meiji who finally came to power in 1868 Japan witnessed a rapid modernization from 'backwater feudal isola-tion' to 'Great Power' status in just 50 years. The Meiji period saw an infatuation with Western culture. Staggeringly, in less than half a century Japan had absorbed and indigenized virtu-ally the entire technical inheritance of the Western world up to graduate level.[41] During this second opening up American Protestant missionaries came to the fore. It was this second opening up that brought the gospel to Koyama's own family. Mr Herbert George Brand (1865–1942), a layman and grad-uate of Cambridge, came to Japan in 1888, not sent by any mission body. Koyama recalls that 'the gospel of Jesus Christ which my grandfather heard was presented in broken Japanese with a heavy English accent. What a moment of inspiration to hear the gospel in a broken language.'[42] Perhaps Koyama understood the weakness, vulnerability and 'inefficacy' of Mr Brand with a fondness as he too knew the 'inefficiency' of his own language-learning ability in Thailand.

It was during the turn of the nineteenth century when Koyama's paternal grandfather accepted the gospel and Japan was in transition. The modernization pursued by Emperor Meiji reflected the preoccupations of Europe and North America at the time: the building of railways, introduction of a central bank, compulsory education, national service, etc. But the cry of *Fukoku Kyohei* ('Enrich the Country, Strengthen the Military') contained the seeds of Japanese imperialism and militarism leading to Japan's victory over China in the first Sino-Japanese war (1894–5) and later victory over Russia

(1904–5). This transition was not without its dark side. Opposition was crushed, parts of the natural environment desecrated, and elements of noble society were marginalized. For Koyama, the Meiji government launched a massive and aggressive campaign to establish the 'divinity' of the emperor. It was on this basis that Japan declared war on the USA, Great Britain and the Netherlands in 1941. The emperor was presented as god in human form – 'his august glory reached the end of the universe', stated the declaration.

The culmination of Japanese expansionism in 1928–42 included significant parts of north China, and much of southeast Asia stretching into the Philippines and Indonesia until surrender in 1945. That surrender was initiated by the utter atomic destruction of Hiroshima on 6 August, Nagasaki three days later, and finally Emperor Hirohito's admission of defeat on 15 August. For Koyama, the cult of emperor worship was defeated in these moments,[43] and such moments are what Koyama has called the 'discontinuity' between pre-war and post-war life.[44]

Bushido

I think some elements of the Samurai warrior code can be detected in the theology of Koyama. But perhaps that is not saying much as this honour code is deeply embedded in wider Japanese culture. When feudalism was formally inaugurated a warrior class came to the fore, most especially during the period when Japan was cut off from the rest of the world. The Bushido is the set of moral principles that the Samurai were required to observe. Not written down but passed along via a few maxims, Nitobe says many aspects of Bushido's origins are rooted in Buddhism: 'Its sense of calm trust in fate, quiet submission to the inevitable and stoic composure in the slight of danger or calamity.'[45] These aspects were loyalty, self-sacrifice, sincerity, frugality, integrity, non-attachment to life, honour in the face of death, humility and compassion. It's not hard to see how the themes that Koyama picks up on in his theology are echoed in Bushido. For example, the self-denial, self-sacrifice, integrity, and facing death with honour are clearly bound up in the narratives of Jesus of Nazareth.

Mingei

It may too be possible to detect elements of the *Mingei* movement in Koyama's theologizing. *Mingei* was a folk-craft movement initiated by Yanagi Soētsu in the early 1920s and had a profound influence not only on Japan but also the wider international art and crafts scene, most notably the St Ives-based potter Bernard Leach. *Mingei* was a recovery of simple, utilitarian craft pieces, everyday objects to be used in the homes of ordinary people. Most often there was no stamp to indicate who had made the piece. It remained anonymous. Its gift was simply to do its job. The way of *mingei* was not self-power of self-assertion. It was also to some extent a reaction to Japanese appropriation of Western technology, power and mass production which really came to the fore after World War Two. Again, it is easy to see how Koyama's reaction to technology, speed and power might have been subtly influenced by the *Mingei* movement.

Koyama in ecumenical and World Christianity contexts

Koyama played a vital role in the ecumenical movement. For a number of years at the WCC he participated in groups such as Faith and Order, Human Studies, the Dialogue with People of Other Faiths and Ideologies, Church and Society, the Nairobi Assembly, and the commission on World Mission and Evangelism. But he was also a prominent figure in the emerging World Christianity movement. Dale Irvin says that, 'Koyama felt the pulse of resurgence of Christianity around the world at a time when others were sceptical about its future and even of the prospects of religion in general in the West. He brought a largeness of heart, mind, and soul to bear on urgent issues confronting World Christianity and the ecumenical movement.'[46]

The modern ecumenical mission movement is generally traced back to the World Missionary Conference in Edinburgh in 1910. This was a gathering born out of the vision of John Mott from the Student Christian Movement who was recognized as the undisputed leader of the ecumenical missionary movement for 40 years.[47] The range of its participants, the breadth and depth of its enquiry, and the scale of its ambition were notable. Its participants were drawn from British and American Protestant mission agencies. The language and optimism of the conference seems to ring hollow now. There was much talk of 'decisive hour', 'this generation' and 'opportunities' – but this conference buoyant with enthusiasm was about to be shattered by World War One. In 1921 the International Missionary Council (IMC) was formed but it was unable to meet until the follow-up conference which took place in Jerusalem in 1928. By that point, everything had changed. David Bosch says that at this conference, 'for the first time there was a realisation that Christianity was no Western religion and that the West was not Christian in its entirety. Its spiritual poverty was evident to all.'[48] Further conferences met in 1938 at Tambaram in India, whose central theme was 'witness', and again at Whitby in 1947 and Willingen in 1952.[49]

It was at Willingen that a 'missiological turn' took place. Perhaps it was more obvious in 1952 with Mao Tse Tung's victory in China and the death, imprisonment and exile of all Western missionaries that 'a fundamental revolution had taken place in the world. It became increasingly clear that the starting point for a theology of mission was not to be found in the church but in God himself. To put it differently: mission should not be based on ecclesiology but on Christology.'[50] But it was at Willingen that a more trinitarian focus on mission arose. The classical doctrine of *missio Dei* as God the Father sending the Son, and God the Father and the Son sending the

Spirit, was expanded into yet another movement: Father, Son and Spirit sending the Church into the world. The Triune community overflows and outflows with love for the other. *Missio Dei* reminds us that the Church is the Church for others: kenotic, selfless, outpouring. We are invited into the life of the Godhead. The Father, Son and Spirit are a community in communion.

The last meeting of the IMC convened in Ghana in 1958 before finally being absorbed into the WCC in New Delhi in 1961. Both Max Warren, General Secretary of Church Mission Society (CMS), and Ralph Winter saw this integration as a mistake. Kim says, 'Rather than putting mission at the heart of the church, some feared that "evangelical zeal" would be sacrificed for the sake of "nominal unity".'[51]

Warren believed that the integration of the IMC into the WCC was an institutionalization, looking for solutions in structures and imprisoning the Holy Spirit. This integration also left many missionary agencies without a mutual bond since the WCC was a council of churches, not parachurch organizations. However, there were advantages in the integration as Kim points out: 'although the WCC was not a church and the IMC was not a mission, the merger of the two was also intentionally illustrative of the desirability of the integration of church and mission'.[52]

As a result of this, and the growing concern from evangelicals around the WCC's liberal orientation, preparations for a new congress emerged. The first International Congress on World Evangelization (ICOWE) took place in Lausanne, Switzerland, in July 1974. The gathering was called by a committee headed by the Revd Billy Graham and drew more than 2,300 evangelical leaders from 150 countries.

The tension between the WCC and the Lausanne Movement has been well documented. Both the WCC Commission on World Mission and Evangelism and the Lausanne Movement saw themselves as the legitimate heirs of the 1910 World Missionary Conference in Edinburgh. Hart has noted that 'in place of regular worldwide mission conferences, there emerged

two distinct and often mutually antagonistic mission movements claiming the mandate of 1910'.[53] In a 1981 article,
Bosch includes an insightful reflection on the creation-centred
approach and the redemption-centred perspective via major
mission conferences in Melbourne (May 1980) and Pattaya
(June 1980). This essentially highlighted the gulf between
the WWC Commission on World Mission and Evangelism,
which is generally ecumenical, over and against the Lausanne
Movement which was specifically evangelical. These differences
are highlighted in the table below:

Melbourne (WWC)	Pattaya (Lausanne)
Hears the cry of the poor and oppressed	Hears the cry of the lost
Considers man from the perspective of creation	Considers man from the perspective of the fall
Judges the world positively	Judges the world negatively
No clear boundaries between church and world	The boundaries between church and world are clear
Regards the world as the main arena of God's activity	Regards the Church as the main arena of God's activity

Table taken from D. Bosch, 1981, 'In Search of Mission: Reflections
on "Melbourne" and "Pattaya"', *Missionalia* 9(1), p. 5, used with
permission.

Hunt writes, 'From the 1950s to the 1970s the WCC moved
toward expansive understandings of the *missio Dei*, the
"mission/sending of God," that could include much more than
personal evangelism in the Christian mandate. Such understandings addressed the crisis of a mission that was seen as too
narrow to address the challenges of the postcolonial world.'[54]
Pachuau points out, somewhat unfairly, that 'The World
Council of Churches failed to characterize "world Christianity." The Council's positioning has become rather passive on

missionary expansion and practically discarded the importance of numerical growth of the church, especially since the
1960s. This apparent lack of missionary zeal dissociated the
council from the major growth of Christianity in the Southern
hemispheres.'[55]

Koyama played a particularly important role in the 1980
WCC conference in Melbourne, yet parallel to that conference the Lausanne Movement was hosting a congress of world
evangelization in Pattaya, Thailand. It seems ironic that while
the WCC and the Lausanne Movement were often, during
those parallel meetings in 1974, 1980 and 1989, in tension
with each other, Koyama's commitment to *theologia crucis*,
humility and love of Scripture, could have helped bridge the
divide. Today, people like Kirsteen Kim are an example of
those who work both within the Lausanne Movement and the
WCC, happily bridging the historic divide. There is much less
suspicion between the movements today. Indeed, in the most
recent major statement from the WCC, *Together Towards Life*,
Jooseop Keum notes that 'a growing intensity of collaboration
with Evangelicals, especially with the Lausanne Movement for
World Evangelization and the World Evangelical Alliance, has
also abundantly contributed to the enrichment of ecumenical
theological reflection on mission in unity'.[56] In fact, 'it is ques-
tionable whether the dichotomy of ecumenical and evangelical
perspectives is still relevant to envisioning the future of world
Christianity'.[57]

Koyama naturally seems to be what Bosch called a 'pan
Christian'. In 1988, outlining the relationship between ecumenical and evangelicals, he wrote, 'What we really need,
however, and need desperately, is what Nathan Söderblom
once called "pan-Christians", people who stand for the whole-
ness and fullness of the gospel and refuse to allow phrases such
as "evangelical", "ecumenical", "catholic", and "charismatic"
to be downgraded to party terms and become the monopoly
of only one group.'[58] In Bosch's subsequent list of who might
be deemed a 'pan-Christian', Koyama doesn't appear but
then nor does Bosch who was certainly seen as someone who

was respected and valued by both constituencies. Koyama was a bridge builder, pronouncing a kind prophetic humility resolutely committed to Scripture and deeply aware of context.

Conclusion

Each chapter in this book takes a particular theme from Koyama's writing that speaks into the current climate of mission in the UK but also frames it in terms of a journey with Jesus through his life, death and resurrection.

The title of Chapter 2 is 'Walking'. We ask questions about the relationship between walking, slowness, time and speed and whether we are operating out of an existential anxiety about the future Church and therefore expect shorter and shorter timeframes for growth. In this chapter I ask if the Church of England's resource church 'model' is caught up in an unhelpful urgency.

In Chapter 3, titled 'Seeing', I consider the Church and its mission legacy as deeply connected to an appalling record of imperialistic violence and empire building. I ask how Koyama's concepts of 'neighbourology' and hospitality to strangers could be useful starting points for undoing some of that and might enable us to 'see' ourselves and others better. I consider the gift of migration into the UK of Christians from across the globe as a way of both challenging and renewing our lives together. I share two stories of Christians who have made their home in the UK, and their experiences, and consider what a future intercultural Church might look like.

In Chapter 4, 'Talking', we explore the theme of evangelism in the UK through the lens of Koyama who felt that Christianity was in danger of becoming irrelevant because it suffered from what he called 'teacher complex'. The chapter unpacks the notion of evangelism as listening and the ideas of 'spat-upon' and 'stigma' evangelism in a world full of words, power and a love for the spectacular.

'Surrendering', Chapter 5, considers how Jesus surrendered

himself to powerlessness and explores the way in which the Church, at various times in its history, has struggled with relinquishing temporal power, and how its leaders have time and again given in to the temptation of embracing. The chapter explores the idea of surrender and immobility and also the relationship between technology and the 'inefficient one'. I explore the potential dangers of transhumanism and the gift of the digital church.

Chapter 6, the concluding chapter, is titled 'In Him All Things Hold Together'. It draws together some of the key themes and asks pertinent questions from the preceding chapters, and finishes by considering Koyama's insistence that the ecumenical movement will only continue to be vital if it keeps Jesus Christ the crucified one at the centre of its theology and worship.

Each chapter begins with a short reflection on Jesus' ministry before moving on to explore that theme in dialogue with Koyama's writing. The overriding theme is that of slowing down, since all the other parts of reflecting on mission with Koyama are predicated on slowing down and therefore being able to attend to what is important.

Notes

1 A Cambodian term for foreigner.

2 D. Day, 1940, 'Aims and Purposes (1940)', *The Catholic Worker Movement*, https://www.catholicworker.org/dorothyday/articles/182. html, accessed 22.3.2022.

3 CTE is the national ecumenical instrument supporting and encouraging churches from a wide range of traditions to work together in unity. See www.cte.org.uk.

4 K. Koyama, 1980, 'The Crucified Christ Challenges Human Power' in *Your Kingdom Come: Mission Perspectives – Report on the World Conference of Mission and Evangelism*, Geneva: WCC Publications.

5 D. Shriver, 1996, 'An Afterword' in D. Irvin and A. Akinade, *The Agitated Mind of God: The Theology of Kosuke Koyama*, Maryknoll, NY: Orbis Books, p. 229.

6 For a systematic and thorough approach to Koyama, see M. Morse, 1991, *Kosuke Koyama: A Model for Intercultural Theology*, Frankfurt am Main: Peter Lang.

7 S. Bevans and R. Schroeder, 2011, *Prophetic Dialogue on Christian Mission Today*, Maryknoll, NY: Orbis Books.

8 V. Erickson, 1996, 'Neighborology: A Feminist Ethno-Missiological Celebration of Kosuke Koyama' in D. Irvin and A. Akinade (eds), *The Agitated Mind of God: The Theology of Kosuke Koyama*, Maryknoll, NY: Orbis Books, p. 152.

9 K. Koyama, 1974, *Waterbuffalo Theology*, London: SCM Press, p. viii.

10 K. Koyama, 1997, 'My Pilgrimage in Mission', *International Bulletin of Missionary Research* 21(2), p. 55.

11 Koyama, 'My Pilgrimage in Mission', p. 55.

12 Koyama, 'My Pilgrimage in Mission', p. 55.

13 Koyama, 'My Pilgrimage in Mission', p. 56.

14 K. Koyama, 1984, *Mount Fuji and Mount Sinai: A Pilgrimage in Theology*, London: SCM Press.

15 K. Koyama, 1980, 'The Crucified Christ Challenges Human Power' in *Your Kingdom Come: Mission Perspectives – Report on the World Conference of Mission and Evangelism*, Geneva: WCC Publications, pp. 157–70.

16 K. Koyama, 1979, *Three Mile an Hour God*, London: SCM Press, p. 13.

17 S. B. Bevans, 1985, 'Models of Contextual Theology', *Missiology: An International Review*, 13(2), pp. 185–202.

18 S. B. Bevans and K. Tahaafe-Williams (eds), 2011, *Contextual Theology for the Twenty-First Century*, Eugene, OR: Pickwick Publications, p. 12.

19 S. B. Bevans, 2002, *Models of Contextual Theology*, Maryknoll, NY: Orbis Books, p. 21.

20 Bevans, *Models of Contextual Theology*, p. 21.

21 Bevans, *Models of Contextual Theology*, p. 21.

22 Bevans, *Models of Contextual Theology*, p. 37.

23 Bevans, *Models of Contextual Theology*, p. 55.

24 Bevans, *Models of Contextual Theology*, p. 89.

25 Bevans, *Models of Contextual Theology*, p. 97.

26 Koyama, *Waterbuffalo Theology*, pp. 78ff.

27 Koyama, *Waterbuffalo Theology*, p. 82.

28 K. Koyama, 1977, *No Handle on the Cross: An Asian Meditation on the Crucified Mind*, Eugene, OR: Wipf and Stock, p. 69.

29 Koyama, *No Handle on the Cross*, p. 71.

30 Koyama, *No Handle on the Cross*, p. 71.

31 Koyama, *Mount Fuji and Mount Sinai*, p. 16.

32 John A. Kohan, 2011, 'Profound Faith, Profound Beauty: The Life and Art of Sadao Watanabe', *Image* 74, https://imagejournal.org/article/profound-faith-profound-beauty-life-art-sadao-watanabe/, accessed 23.3.2022.

33 Kohan, 'Profound Faith, Profound Beauty'.

34 K. Koyama, 1975, '"Not by Bread Alone..." How Does Jesus Free Us and Unite Us?', *The Ecumenical Review*, 24(3), p. 201.

35 It is obviously impossible to squeeze the entire history of Christianity in Japan and theologians into the space of this book. This is a brief outline. For more on how Koyama relates the Japanese theology, read chapter 2 of M. Morse, 1991, *Kosuke Koyama: A Model for Intercultural Theology*, Bern: Peter Lang, pp. 37ff.

36 Morse, *Kosuke Koyama*, p. 55.

37 Morse, *Kosuke Koyama*, p. 21.

38 Koyama, *Three Mile an Hour God*, pp. 83–111.

39 Koyama, *Three Mile an Hour God*, p. 89.

40 Koyama, *Mount Fuji and Mount Sinai*, p. 169.

41 R. Tames, 2002, *A Traveller's History of Japan*, London: Cassell & Co., p. 132.

42 Koyama, *Mount Fuji and Mount Sinai*, p. 15.

43 Koyama, *Three Mile an Hour God*, p. 102.

44 Koyama, *Waterbuffalo Theology*, p. 17.

45 Koyama, *Waterbuffalo Theology*, p. 12.

46 D. Irvin and A. Akinade, 2009, 'Rejoicing in Hope: A Tribute to Kosuke Koyama', *International Bulletin of Missionary Research*, 33(3), p. 139.

47 D. Bosch, 1980, *Witness to the World: The Christian Mission in Theological Perspective*, Eugene, OR: Wipf & Stock, p. 159.

48 Bosch, *Witness to the World*, p. 161.

49 An excellent overview of these conferences from 1910 to 1952 can be found in Bosch, *Witness to the World*, pp. 159–81.

50 Bosch, *Witness to the World*, p. 178.

51 K. Kim, 2020, 'Mission: Integrated or Autonomous? Implications for the Study of World Christianity' in A. Chow and E. Wild-Wood (eds), *Ecumenism and Independency in World Christianity: Historical Studies in Honour of Brian Stanley*, Leiden: Brill, p. 65.

52 Kim, 'Mission: Integrated or Autonomous?', p. 67.

53 H. A. Hunt, 2011, 'The History of the Lausanne Movement, 1974–1989', *International Review of Missionary Research*, 35(2), pp. 81–4.

54 Hunt, 'The History of the Lausanne Movement, 1974–1989', p. 81.

55 L. Pachuau, 2018, *World Christianity: A Historical and Theological Introduction*, Nashville, TN: Abingdon Press, p. 6.

56 J. Keum, (ed), 2013, *Together Towards Life: Mission and Evangelism in Changing Landscapes*, Geneva: WCC Publications, p. 24.

57 J. Keum, 2016, 'Conclusion – Together in God's Mission: Prospects for Ecumenical Missiology' in K. Ross, J. Keum, K. Avtzi and R. Hewitt, *Ecumenical Missiology: Changing Landscapes and New Conceptions of Mission*, Oxford: Regnum, p. 572.

58 D. Bosch, 1988, '"Ecumenicals" and "Evangelicals": A Growing Relationship?', *The Ecumenical Review*, 40(3–4), p. 472.

2

Walking:
The Importance of Slowing Down

Jesus walking in the New Testament

Jesus never seemed to be in a rush, but was never late. He was late to heal Lazarus, who then died, but was on time to raise him from the dead. He often changed his direction, was interrupted or seemingly re-routed, yet Jesus revealed aspects of his divinity that would otherwise have been hidden. He worked on a timeframe that confused others.

During his ministry Jesus covered very little ground from any modern perspective. An early cross-border interlude into Egypt was the extent of his 'international' travel. Most of his early experience was shaped by his time in Nazareth, his childhood home. Matthew's Gospel gives us a good indication of where he went and what he did. From his birthplace in Bethlehem, to healing the Gentile woman's daughter in Tyre (his most northerly exploit), Jesus spent much of his life being attentive to the needs of those on his doorstep. The incarnate God felt no need to run. He was not in a hurry. He was slow but never slothful. He allowed himself to be continually interrupted but this did not deflect him from his ultimate purpose to be fulfilled in Jerusalem. He was purposeful but also 'time*full*'. He was unhurried. He did the thing that was in front of him with his full attention.

He took a painful and slow route to Golgotha, bearing the weight of a roughly cut cross. After his death and resurrection, we only have a few examples of his walking. One that stands out is found in Luke 24.13–34 where Jesus accompanies two of his followers, explaining to them all the things concerning himself from the Scriptures. It was only as they sat with him in their home and broke bread that suddenly their eyes were opened, and their hearts burned within them.

And then he promptly disappeared.

Many of us struggle to live in this Christ 'time*full*ness'. We resist allowing life and ministry to unfold at a walking pace, to be unhurried. Koyama's aphorism of the 'Three Mile an Hour God' has in many ways become eponymous with his theology. It permeates almost all that he wrote. It encompasses a theological posture that acts as a counter narrative to pace, power and prestige, all of which Koyama found anathema to being a Christ follower.

Koyama wrestled for much of his theological life with idolatry, which he found most closely in the history of his own nation of Japan and the near total destruction of Tokyo, which he witnessed first-hand as a teenager. It was his reflections on idolatry and destruction that humbled him and 'slowed me down'.[1] Koyama wrote about the God who walked slowly, who takes time and is time*full*. So perhaps it will help us to explore walking, time and speed and the ways in which they impact our approaches to mission and ministry.

Going for a walk

In early December 2020, I left the shackles of my study desk and went for a walk. I've had a dream for a long time of walking the entire South West Coast Path. It's the longest way-marked footpath in England, stretching from Minehead in north Devon round Cornwall (my homeland) and eventually arriving at Poole in Dorset; the path is a significant 630 miles of beautiful and dramatic landscape.

On this particular winter morning, I left my house in Sidmouth and walked the 14 miles along the coast to Exmouth. Sitting low in the sky, the sun dazzled me as it reflected off the sea. Following the footpath is not simply walking along

expansive vistas of cliff tops facing luminescent sea. The contours of the path led me through scrubby pine forest, sheer
descents into tiny valleys cut by streams and via old crumbly
roads. Although always aware of the sea, at times I simply
could not see it. The path coerced me into deep muddy tracks
with gorse so thick I could not see through, but I could hear the
ocean lapping at a remote shingle beach below. And although
I was vaguely aware of my destination it wasn't the objective.
Enjoying the path was.

Because we are so often focused on our destination we can
miss what may be in a hedgerow, or an unexpected sight at the
side of the road, in a field, or what might be at the end of a
track. During our first six months in Cambodia in early 2005
my wife Sharon and I took a long and very slow journey from
Phnom Penh up Highway 7 through Kracheh and onwards to
Stung Treng near the Laos border before boarding a small boat
along with a number of schoolchildren travelling back to their
village of Siem Pang. It took us days. Finally, we hopped on
the back of a motorbike through the stubby fields to a tiny
community mostly made up of ex-Khmer Rouge fighters who
had been given remote scraps of land as part of a peace agreement in the early 1990s. The last part of that journey required
us to walk as even motorbikes struggled to handle the rough
terrain. Everyone entered that community on foot. To enter
a place on foot with only a simple bag is to come in some
degree of vulnerability. For three days we ate, slept, washed,
sang, prayed, listened (difficult when you only have six months
of language study under your belt) and attempted to teach
something.

Each morning a young man in his thirties desperate to learn
to play the keyboard would wait at the bottom of a stepladder
of the house I was staying in (all traditional Cambodian
houses are built on stilts 9 feet off the ground to avoid the
flood waters). He was an ex-Khmer Rouge soldier and had
mahogany-coloured skin and gnarled hands from a life of
what I presumed to be fighting and farming. He had obtained
a small Chinese manufactured electronic keyboard of about

two octaves and one sound – a sort of distorted sine wave. It was and still is the most appalling keyboard sound I have ever had the misfortune of hearing or playing. As there was no electricity in the village (or running water) he had ingeniously wired the keyboard up to a car battery and every morning and afternoon I would attempt to teach him the melody of a well-known Cambodian Christian hymn. I think it is fair to say he was not a natural musician. By the third morning he had mastered the first line – from my perspective it was not going well. I had to literally hold his finger over each key and press it down at the correct moment during most of our teaching sessions. But when he managed falteringly to play part of the melody back to me as we were getting ready to leave, his smile – teeth missing and all – I will never forget. All because, in a sense, we had to walk in and had been slowed down by the process. Sometimes we need to be slowed down in order just to show up. A former Khmer Rouge soldier who had begun the journey of following Jesus some months previously could play a line of music for his church ... sometime in the future.

Perhaps following the footpaths or trails is a metaphor for joining God in God's mission to the world? Much of the mundaneness of ministry is where God is slowly shaping us through one another, quietly honing us, working on us. But we must slow down to walking speed to notice.

Homo sapiens has always walked. In Sanskrit, one of the world's oldest languages originating in India, the past tense is designated by the word *gata* which means 'that which we have walked'.

Throughout the ages, philosophers have known the wisdom to be found in and through walking: 'the rhythm of walking generates a kind of rhythm of thinking'.[2] In a Western culture obsessed with productivity, results, objectives and targets, going for a walk to think is problematic since doing nothing is hard to do. Yet walking is as natural as breathing and sleeping. It's something we are designed to do and so we do it subconsciously.

Walking slows us down. It liberates us from the tyranny of the urgent, anxiety-inducing posture of our multitasking culture. But walking is complex. There are times when we walk in purposeful and determined ways; we are aware of our gait. Other times we walk head down, bumbling and muddling our way towards our destination. Sometimes it feels like life is one long plod.

Walking and plodding

When we drive on a motorway it's impossible to see much of what is happening at the side of the road. Walking has revealed to me over the years parts of places, cities, towns and villages I would never have seen or encountered. Walking helps us to notice. When we walk we simply can't go fast. Going fast is called running. But walking can elicit bemused and disconcerting responses. At the congregation I served in Cape Town in 2013–18 one of the church members told me he didn't like seeing his minister walking. Ministers in African culture are status symbols – they should drive around in a Toyota Corolla or some such equivalent! It showed that the congregation are looking after clergy. Walking was considered a slap in the face.

When my youngest daughter was two, I would take her for a walk about three mornings a week. She didn't like to walk as I do. If I walk alone, I walk fast. When I'm in London for work I try to walk from King's Cross station to my office in Euston as fast as possible. I pick people out of the crowd and mentally pit myself against them, seeing if I can overtake them in my imagined race. My walk with my daughter could best be described as inefficient. I waited, and sometimes cajoled her to walk. She wanted to stop often. She sometimes walked back up the hill when I wanted to go down. She dawdled, pulled at plants and flowers growing out of the wall. She refused to go at my pace even when I held her hand and 'marched' her along. She forced me to slow down. To breathe. To go at her pace. To figure out what she was so curious about. Relationship with her forced me to do that. My responsibility for her compelled me to learn to go slow.

Walking is not a sport. Walking enables us – or perhaps forces us – into a different rhythm. Koyama says:

> when we walk (three miles an hour) we see many things, we feel wind, we feel rain, we are warmed by sunshine, we can smell the pleasant aromas as we pass food stalls. We are not shut up. We are not rushing at fifty miles an hour. Our pace is three miles an hour on our own feet.[3]

'If you want to go faster, don't walk', says Frédéric Gros, 'do something else: drive, slide or fly. Don't walk. And when you are walking there is only one sort of performance that counts; the brilliance of the sky, the splendour of the landscape.'[4]

Sometimes life includes a type of walking we would call a plod. It is simply about putting one foot in front of the other. Simply progressing along the way a little further than yesterday and in the process feeding the children, hoovering the carpet, preparing food, paying a bill, changing a nappy, wiping up the vomit or remembering the washing machine is still leaking. In plodding we are journeying along the road which continues to call us to what is, as Eugene Peterson famously said, 'a long obedience in the same direction'.

Walking slowly in time

If we are going to think about walking and slowness then we need also to think about time. Slowness is relative to people's experience.

In 1996 I spent a summer in Jinja, Uganda, with Youth With A Mission. It was my first experience of life on the African continent. As you might imagine, the pace and rhythm of life was different to anything I had experienced. I was used to church beginning at precisely 10.30 a.m. whether there were 100 people sitting in the well-oiled pews or only 10. I remember each of the team being asked to preach in different village churches across the area. Dressed in my tie with my smartly polished shoes and *Life Application Bible* under my arm, I anticipated an expectant crowd ready to listen to my fine sermon full of exegetical gems. When we arrived at 10.30 there was only a handful of women and their children sitting in silence. The church with its rusting corrugated iron roof was cavernous and could hold at least 200 people. Over the next hour and a half people began to trickle in and things eventually got going by midday.

In my Western experience the important thing was starting on time. In the Ugandan context the important thing was starting when everyone had arrived. In the Western context we have become slaves of clock time: I *will* start my service at 10.30 regardless of whether there are people present or not. In the Ugandan context, people come first and the start time is a secondary consideration. Events start when everyone is present.

Time is an elusive thing. Although we live in time, our hearts long for a future where we are not hemmed in by it. Eternity is written on and in our hearts.[5] Our perceptions of time change depending on our age and circumstances. We want holiday time to unfold slowly but time under the dentist's drill to go quickly. As children we enjoy the summer evenings which seem to carry on for ever as we play. A prisoner in solitary confinement experiences time like a heavy weight carried day after weary day, marking the days until finally released.[6] Patients in hospital often speak of time feeling different to the outside world, as if they are in some kind of alternate time zone. A popular bumper sticker on the back of cars in the 1990s in the south-west of England was 'Driving slows down in Devon'. A friend moved to the area from London and was infuriated by the speed at which people drove. What one person considers slow may in fact be quite fast and vice versa.

Western ideas of time are often a fragmented series of tiny shards. Cleaning teeth – 1 minute 23 seconds. Drying dishes – 3 minutes 16 seconds. Changing child's nappy – too much time! John Swinton says, 'Time is created as a series of dislocated fragmented moments held together by the transient necessities of human desire.'[7] As the atomization in science flowed over into society and culture, we noticed that 'the clockwork of the heavens turned out to be, well, a bit wobbly'.[8] The discovery of the atom led by Niels Bohr and Werner Heisenberg developed into deeper studies around the behaviour of electrons orbiting within a caesium atom. It was noted they rotated with astonishing accuracy, and thus we had the basis for the first atomic clocks.

One result is that our Western obsession with clock time can be linked back to a conference that took place in Paris on 13 October 1967 which gathered leading scientists from across the world. Under the fairly innocuous title of 'The General Conference of Weights and Measures', those gathered made a staggering decision: they agreed to change the very definition of time.[9] In this new era, an atomic second was defined as 'the duration 9,192,631,770 periods of radiation corresponding to the transition between the two hyperfine levels of the ground state of the caesium 133 atom'.[10] Atomic time, while the pinnacle of scientific observation, has drawn us into an unhelpful (and at times unhealthy) relationship with time and led to the change in definition of the value of a second.

In many ways the scientists' decision was the logical conclusion in the age of scientific rationalism. The world had become increasingly shaped by the objectives of enlightenment rationalism: efficiency, calculability, predictability and control.[11] This would shape how we understand and measure everything, even time.

That world of astonishing accuracy has led us to believe we can control, bend and shape time. We think about manipulating time. We compartmentalize our day into chunks of time. There is nothing more frowned upon by the busy Kantian work ethic puritans among us than 'wasting time'. In our family we start our home day with our family at 8 a.m. and we are usually shouting to our oldest girls to get out of the shower and get to the library. Do we think we can bend and shape time with our shouts?

Our lives in the twenty-first century have not only been shaped by the mantras of scientific rationalism but by economic factors too. We are hassled by truisms such as 'time is money and money is time'. Begbie acknowledges that 'the history of capitalism has been characterised by a speed up in the pace of life, while so overcoming spatial barriers that the world sometimes seems to collapse inward upon us'.[12]

Carl Honoré notes how mechanical clocks began to be introduced into major European cities in the fourteenth century. Historical records suggest that a public clock was erected in the German city of Cologne around 1370. By 1374 the city had passed a statute that fixed the start and end of the working day for labourers and fixed their lunchtime as 'one hour and no longer'. Within one generation the people of Cologne went from never knowing for sure what time it was to allowing the clock to dictate the entire rhythm of their lives.[13]

That fourteenth-century shift continued until the beginning of the Industrial Revolution which was fed on a 'diet speed'. Lewis Mumford the eminent social critic said that the key machine of the Industrial Revolution was the clock. The clock promised to revolutionize stragglers and 'behind time' people. The mechanization of work, the paramount importance that an individual make a certain number of widgets per hour drove economics. People were commodified – their value inextricably linked to what they could produce.

But at the beginning of the twentieth century these obsessions crept into other parts of culture. The Italian Futurist movement launched their manifesto in 1909 with a utopian vision of a never-tiring humankind in perpetual motion. 'We declare that the splendour of the world has been enriched by a new beauty: the beauty of speed.'[14] And so the global capitalist economy has compressed time and space in ways that have increasingly led us to despair – longer working hours, less rest and more impossible demands. The rhythm of work and rest woven into the fabric of creation and the story of God's people has been rejected in favour of a 24-hour, never stopping, always shopping, life.

A recent story of delivery drivers in South Korea reveals the significance of this:

> It was an hour before sunrise, 21 hours into a shift, and Mr Kim had delivered more than 400 packages. The 36-year-old delivery driver had been working since 5 a.m. the previous day. He messaged a colleague, pleading to skip a round of parcel deliveries. 'It's too much,' he wrote. 'I just can't.' Four days later, Mr Kim was dead.[15]

That story reveals the worst of zero-hours contracts and the insatiable demands for goods and products in shorter and shorter timescales. It is the pinnacle of never-stopping-never-resting speed. In a culture where our relationship with time has become more and more toxic, where the need for rest and healthy rhythms in daily life have been squeezed and squashed, we see the results in exhaustion and death. And yet ideas and perceptions of time are shaped by our own cultural vantage point. Our Western preoccupation with minutes and seconds – in short, exactitude – is not replicated in other places.

Koyama wrote that our obsessions with manipulating or mastering time are rooted ultimately in selfishness and greed. 'My greed will dictate my relationship with time. The selfish use of time will bring spiritual destruction. Somehow selfish time is destructive. I must be able to abandon *thirsting* after self importance.'[16]

God and time

How then can we learn to live in Christ's timefullness as a counter narrative to the preoccupation with clock time and the speed that we see in action all around us? Jeremy Begbie says, 'Christ's time and history, his incarnate life, death and resurrection, are thus properly conceived as central and decisive for all time and history.'[17] Christ acts as the bookends of history and invites us to live time-full lives because history is in his hands. The one who flung stars into space holds time in his hands. We can receive the gift of time from him along with his gift of life. Perhaps it's easiest to think of time as something that, as Swinton says, 'came into existence with the advent of creation'. Since the world was created as a relational act by the community, in communion time might be best seen not as 'an impersonal, free-floating commodity intended for the satiation of human desire but as an aspect of God's relationship to the world'.[18]

The God of the Bible is presented as eternal. God does not grow weary or old; God's years are without end. To speak of God as timeless makes God immutable. Might it be better to consider God as time*full*? The God of Scripture is the God of the living who choses to accompany people throughout history and is intimately involved with people in 'real time'.

Augustine and time

Theologians and philosophers have through the ages reflected upon time, and debated its meaning and constitution. Augustine was perhaps the first to reflect on the nature of time in any extensive way. He was the first to devise a philosophy of time; a subjective approach to time rather than the technical understanding of it that has come to dominate our understanding from Einstein onwards. As you might expect, Augustine's reflections on time are confessional and very much couched in praise and adulation. These reflections on time mostly take place in the second part of Book XI of his *Confessions*.

In Book XI of his *Confessions* Augustine reflects on God and the nature of time by asking 'what then is time?' and is prepared to admit that if asked to explain it he is baffled.[19] Jeremy Begbie reminds us that 'Augustine was affected by a basic conviction of Neoplatonic metaphysics, that "true" existence is immutable existence.' So, for Augustine, timeless entities exist more genuinely than temporary ones. Augustine wonders, 'what was God doing before he made heaven and earth?' and answers, 'He was preparing hell for people who pry into [such] mysteries.'[20] Augustine believed that time is creaturely and that to ask the question what was God doing before time is nonsensical since God doesn't exist in time in the same way that we do. Time comes to us from the future by way of the present and flows into the past. That time exists somehow through *memory* we learn also from St Augustine. After showing that the only time that has any *real existence* is the present moment, he offers another way of explaining time. 'Perchance it might be fitly said, "There are three times, a present of things past, a present of things present, and a present of things future"' (Book XI, 20).[21]

But what is perhaps more important than any analysis of how time functions is how it might be sanctified. That was certainly the relationship with time that the Benedictines sought to observe. The early Benedictine monks' understanding of time was to enable faithfulness and rhythms for worship. St Benedict himself placed great emphasis on order, and Benedict's rule structured the day into eight canonical hours. Bells were used to note the hour to call the faithful to prayer, but as Swinton points out this wasn't about punctuality, promptness or productivity. Benedictine time was *event* time.[22] Ironically, the original ideas for clock time were around creating rhythms for monks to worship. Keeping an eye on the time of the day was to build a pattern into the day to stop and pray, to say morning, midday and evening prayers. As Swinton says, 'To enable people to structure their lives in ways that were faithful to their beliefs and spiritual way of life.'[23]

In the new era of scientific rationalism Isaac Newton suggested that 'time was the "infinite" place of the succession of things. God, omnipresent in space and time, constitutes duration in space – time and space are aspects of God, at least in the sense that God wholly permeates the infinite containers, time and space which are substantial entities.'[24]

By the early twentieth century, the work of Michelson and Morley had rejected Newton's theory and later Einstein radically reshaped our understand of time and space and how they interrelate. Einstein posited that time is not absolute. That the difference between past, present and future is but a stubborn illusion. Our understandings of time in general discourse had shifted from philosophical and spiritual to technical.

Time, *kairos*, *chronos* and speed

Our modern conceptions of time have caused us to live in ways that pit us against the clock and against ourselves, splintering and fracturing time to squeeze as much out of it as possible; it is viewing time as commodity rather than gift. Caught in a toxic relationship with time, hurrying to do more and more, is a violence against the timefullness that we are created for and called to inhabit.

The French cultural theorist Paul Virilio[25] has written that the dominant form of violence in modernity is speed. On a daily basis the world invites me to worship speed and, since it looks like time is running out for the Church, we had better hurry up and get moving. We are running out of time – or so we are sometimes led to believe. It provokes a question about how fast God is going?

Is God in a hurry?

Is there a sense of urgency in God and the way in which God deals with human beings?

Are there ideas of a slow/fast God of the Scriptures? Indeed, what is the speed of God and how is it related to the *kairos*? These important questions are addressed in this book through the lens, or the hermeneutic, of Kosuke Koyama. Too often in British reflections on missiological and ecclesial problems we go to the standard texts from Europe and North America. As valuable and rich as those sources are, might we turn around, slow down and read something from a part of the world we do not generally consider the crucible for creating theology? Might we heed the words of a prophet from the East to help us deal with our Eurocentric myopia?

Koyama on time

I think that part of Koyama's insistence that we are called to be *time*full was rooted in the dramatic and traumatic experiences during World War Two in Tokyo. He writes, 'on the 25th May 1945, I felt as if chronological time had come to a full stop. I felt as though I was swallowed up by an uncanny and meaningless timelessness. I felt so threatened.' Koyama understood what it meant to be humbled by time through the destruction of his own home and the utter devastation in Hiroshima and Nagasaki a few months later. Those experiences never left him, and they resonated through much of what he wrote in the subsequent years.

'I cannot push around time'[26] – time and slowness

When Jesus came declaring the kingdom was close at hand in Mark chapter 1 he says that the time has come.[27] This phrase is familiar to us and we know that Jesus, in this instance, is using the word *kairos* when he speaks of time. There are two basic words for time in New Testament Greek. *Chronos* is the measurable clock time of seconds, minutes, hours, days, months and years; *chronos* is quantitative. *Kairos*, on the other hand, is qualitative. It refers to a decisive moment, to a specific crisis point, perhaps even an unrepeatable moment that must be acted upon. Jesus' own ministry, suggests Koyama, sees 'Chronos shaken by Kairos'.[28] So, a question we must ask ourselves is how does God act in history? Is God mainly working in and through *kairos* moments or is God most happy and willing to teach us in clock time? Rather than try to argue one way or another from arbitrary gleaning of particular Scriptures, I am going to turn to Koyama's treatment of the idea of time and God's hand at work.

As a true intercultural theologian Koyama starts with the concrete context before moving to text. Over and again through his writings Koyama observes that we live a 'speedy

43

and efficient life'.[29] A life shaped by technology allows us to do things quickly.[30] In fact, Koyama says that often meaning has been subjugated to efficiency and speed. While God in Christ operates undoubtedly in *kairos* categories, we should be careful in concluding this is God's only, or preferred, way of teaching, shaping and living out his covenant with human beings. The advent of technology has given us great power and control over many parts of our lives and it is easy to believe that we can 'push time around'. Koyama suggests that those who want to push time around are doing so through a belief in their own self-importance.

Could it be that the unfolding narrative of God's covenant love flows, by and large, in *chronos* time? That flow is interrupted by *kairos* moments. In the overall arc of salvation history it is the interruption of Jesus Christ that is the ultimate *kairos* moment, but Scripture is punctuated with other *kairos* ruptures. For example, Moses at the burning bush, the parting of the Red Sea, Mount Carmel and other theophanic moments. Surely through history there are generations who only hear the rumours of *kairos* activity and never experience that for themselves? At points in Scripture God seems to work at lightning speed. How else does one explain the phenomenon of Philip being snatched away by the Spirit from the road to Gaza all the way to Azotus? Sixty-two miles in a few seconds?[31]

But perhaps it is in the ordinariness of *chronos* time where God works; in, through, and – at times – against people, in the slowness and the mundaneness of clock time. This seems to be what Koyama is alluding to in some of his writing. Koyama reminds us that 'we cannot push time around'. Pushing time around is actually a form of self-importance or pride, but Koyama says the reality is that time humiliates us. It limits us and pushes us.[32] Therefore we should make sure we live a life 'humbled by time'.[33]

For Koyama, God takes time with us:

I find that God goes 'slowly' with his educational process of man. 'Forty years in the wilderness' points to his basic educational philosophy. Forty years of national migration through the wilderness, three generations of united monarchy, nineteen Kings of Israel (up to 722 BC) and twenty kings of Judah (up to 587 BC), the hosts of prophets and priests, the experience of exile and restoration. Isn't this rather a slow and costly way for God to let his people know the covenant relationship between God and man?[34]

God chooses slowness, chooses to act at walking pace. In an article entitled 'Not by Bread Alone' Koyama says, 'Jesus Christ dislikes speedism and sensationalism.'[35] He argues that it is in fact the devil's theology that operates with 'sensational results and speedy solutions'.[36] Many parts of contemporary society, though, are advocating for an alternative narrative to the speed, power and success of the global capitalist economy. The interruption to our lives of the coronavirus pandemic caused many of us to stop. We were encouraged to stay at home, save lives and protect the NHS. We were forced to reconsider where we go, how we go and why we go, but perhaps also how fast we go. It invited us to slow down, to stop. To live at a new pace. At walking pace. An incarnational pace. If science, economics and culture have urged us towards speed, perhaps we need an approach to mission where our ambition is tempered by a life 'humbled by time'.

Koyama and walking

Koyama says that God walks slowly because he is love. The resource church 'model' (which I give a full definition of later) attempts to resource in terms of people, plans and pounds but might we take Koyama's caution about our resourcefulness to heart? Koyama says that 'resourcefulness must be theologically judged and contextualised in order to become genuinely resourceful. Resourcefulness must then be crucified. When it is resurrected it will become a "theologically-baptized resourcefulness".'[37] For Koyama, a major problem in Asian mission history was that missionaries' resourcefulness led to an impoverishment of local Christians in the *missio Dei*. The fundamental problem, says Koyama, is that 'resourceful people do not seek help from others. They know exactly what to do. They have better ideas. They have better strategies.' Therein lies the rub. When we know exactly what to do we may as a result find it hard to learn from others, to come in poverty like the crucified Christ with hands open but wounded. To move into the neighbourhood slowly.

Strategic development funding (SDF): a case study in urgency and speed?

Let me share a little vignette. When I returned to the UK in December 2018 I applied for a wide range of ministry posts. One for which I interviewed was Lead Pioneer in a city that I cannot name for reasons that will become clear. As is often expected of projects funded by Strategic Development Funding (SDF), the work looked exciting and visionary. The intended project outcomes were as follows:

1 Create 20 new fresh expressions of church (fxC) launched in **** within three years;
2 Each new fxC to include at least 20 participants;
3 At least 35% of all participants at fxC to be unchurched;
4 25% of all participants at fxC to be under 30 years of age;
5 70% of fxC to be lay led;
6 The support provided for new fxC by the Lead Pioneers and Pioneer Advocates to be consistently assessed as 'good' or 'excellent'.

In the interview I suggested that the outcomes, although laudable, were virtually impossible to achieve in such a short time-frame. One of the interviewers overseeing the SDF strategy did not appreciate my answers, and as a result I didn't get the job although there were other factors involved – not least my unsuitability for the post. More interestingly, when the post was readvertised a few months later all the timeframes had been removed. This raises a number of important questions in an era when most historic churches in the UK are experiencing sustained decline rather than growth and when the buzz words in some church circles are management, marketing and metrics. It appears we are desperately anxious about our future ecclesial existence – what Alan Roxburgh has described as 'our ecclesiocentric wailing. A sort of protestant flagellation, a myopic guilt atonement, an obsessive preoccupation with dissecting the "church" to name what's wrong and, then, find the technology to fix it one more time.'[38] Is the SDF mechanism, in part, fuelled by this myopic guilt atonement and are we merely using a sticking plaster on a rather deeper wound?

What is SDF and where does it come from?

What is SDF and what is the rationale behind it, particularly at this point in the Church of England's life? The SDF is part of a wider programme in the Church of England for Renewal and Reform. A note at General Synod 2015 from the Archbishops of Canterbury and York says, 'the urgency of the challenge facing us is not in doubt. Attendance at Church of England services has declined at an average of 1% per annum over recent decades and, in addition, the age profile of our membership has become significantly older than that of the population.'[39] The note also set out other challenges around ageing clergy and the burden of church buildings, stating that there needed to be a significant change to the funding mechanisms used by the Church of England to allocate monies to dioceses.

At the General Synod that same year a report from the task force who were asked to look at resourcing the future of the Church of England was given.[40] The report 'proposed a fundamental shift: removing the current formula systems which provide mechanical, ineffective subsidy and replacing them with investment focused on fulfilling dioceses' strategic plans for growth, and with a strong bias towards the poor'.[41] It was a shift from the Darlow formula which 'calculates the needs of parishes based on financial need and attendance. Thus, if attendance in parishes in a diocese decline, the allocation of central funding goes up.'[42] In many respects the report is commendable. It states 'in future, all of the funding distributed to dioceses should be investment for mission and growth'. The report also stated that it wanted to see good growth and recognized that a new formula was needed. While the archbishops said that 'there can be no single strategy for the Church of England's mission and ministry', it certainly seems that there have been particular favourites in terms of models that receive funding – with the 'resource church' model proving the most popular because it seems to guarantee results in relatively short timeframes (a definition of the resource church model follows later in this chapter).

SDF 'supports major change projects which lead to a significant difference in dioceses' mission and financial strength. It is only available to dioceses and the projects should fit with their strategic plans.'[43] A bid process is in place with clear and helpful guidelines and

> SDF has supported a wide range of projects, covering children's and families work; mission to young adults; work addressing deprived areas; pioneer ministry; church planting and fresh expressions of Church; developing leaders for growth; digital evangelism; turnaround work and interim ministry; whole-life discipleship for growth; youth work.[44]

Since its inception, SDF has given out grants ranging from £135,000 (Sodor and Man) to a whopping £8.7 million to the diocese of London in December 2017.

However, as Hilary Davies points out, 'despite a central emphasis on resource churches as centres of generosity, fuelling growth beyond their walls, the source of their rapid growth, and whether the worshipping community is growing as a result, or whether they are concentrating numbers, remains a pressing question'.[45]

I have written elsewhere about SDF and taking culture seriously.[46] I want to extend that and argue that in order to take culture seriously we must drink it in slowly, listen actively and multi-directionally.[47] We must inhabit real timefullness in order to be most effective in the kingdom. The rest of this chapter reflects on the notion of the slowness and inefficiency in relation to mission and SDF resources. SDF has been important in releasing capital for dioceses wishing to try creative things. However, the pressure to successfully increase congregation size in an era when there is an increasing priority on growing churches in smaller and smaller timeframes is problematic. I suggest that reading Koyama may act as an antidote for the preoccupation with speed, size and the spectacular.

In a number of conversations including those with a senior staff member from the Church of England, pioneer and fresh expressions enablers, county ecumenical officers, local denominational leaders and pastors I heard a number of critiques of SDF. Take, for example Charlie,[48] a fresh expressions enabler in a large urban diocese who felt concerned that the bid culture of the Strategic Development Unit (SDU) meant a lot of box ticking shaping a bid around what the funders want and think will work, rather than the particular contextual need of the diocese. He also struggled with the formulaic approach of the SDU. Charlie said,

> Basically, there is formula of cost per disciple. How long to grow a disciple and how much will that cost. If that kind of metric wasn't problematic in and of itself that is linked to a short termism. What will it cost us to make x number of disciples in three years (usual length of the funding)? It's short termism fuelled by the desire for rapid success. It's always focused on the low hanging fruit.

Charlie also expressed anxiety that he spent a third of his time doing evaluation on projects, and was up to his eyes in spreadsheets and forms: 'Always with the sword of Damocles hanging above your head with the threat of funding being removed.' Charlie had 20-plus years of experience pioneering new worshipping communities in parts of the UK's demographic that were currently barely part of the established Church. During the Covid pandemic, he was placed on furlough and ultimately made redundant.

Robert, a senior staff member at Church House who spoke to me on condition of anonymity, gave an insightful and measured response to the SDU but also shared that there was 'growing concern' over how the fund was working. He certainly welcomed the focus on investment rather than subsidy, the need to have greater accountability and actually agreed that there should be some devices for measuring success. There were others who perceived the fund as a great threat to the way the Church had always operated in the parish system and resisted change in any form. Third, there was a group emerging – labelled as 'critical friends' – who wanted to see criticisms of SDF properly addressed.

The first of these issues for Robert was around missiology. He felt there was a lack of structural connection between commissioners of the SDU and those tasked with theologizing in mission. The SDU were essentially pragmatic and spent little time in reflection on how what they were doing was connected to the mission and ministry of the Church. Second, Robert felt that SDF was essentially a series of technical interventions that, because they were limited to three to five years, weren't long enough to bring lasting change. 'In three to five years most things tend simply to fold back into themselves,' he said. Third, in resonance with Charlie, Robert sensed that enormous amounts of money were being spent on project managers, administration and the implementation of funding. Usually, these posts were well above the pay grades of clergy, potentially causing friction between priests in parish settings and those in diocesan or deanery roles seeking to encourage implementation.

Finally, missiologist Wayne observed that bidding for and executing SDF resources has 'skewed' Church of England dioceses into creating projects that need to be centrally appointed and supervised by personnel that go with them. Wayne said that in the worst case scenario dioceses even create projects just to gain the funding. And since everything is formational, it begs the question of what implicit theological formation is going on in SDF work!

This is not to say that the fund, and the vision behind it with its desire to see the Church both flourish and grow numerically, is inherently flawed, but it does reveal what Croatian missiologist Anne-Marie Kool has pointed out as problematic for many churches in late modernity. She argues that they are captive to, 'secular business principles instead of theological principles, focusing more on output and results instead of fruits growing in a hidden way, on value for money instead of free grace, on success stories instead of sacrifice and commitment, on quantity instead of quality, on superficial quick results instead of long-term transformation and incarnation'.[49]

This forces us to ask important questions about how fast we travel, the kind of timeframes we employ, and the type of growth expected. It also provokes us to consider *how* we count and *what* we count.

The 'resource church' model ... a need for speed?

One of the fundamental problems may be that given the short timeframes cited above, many dioceses look to implement a church planting strategy that falls into the reproduction model. The 'resource church' model that is linked to the church revitalization trust[50] is probably the best example of this. Finding a definition of a resource church is difficult. Ric Thorpe defines it as:

A resource church is a church-planting church which re-sources, trains and supports other forms of mission across a city or town. Five core elements define resource churches: they are designated by the diocesan bishop; they are part of a diocesan strategy to evangelise a city or town and transform society; they are intentionally resourced to plant and revitalise churches; they actively develop a pipeline of leaders for further planting; and they provide other resources for mission across their city or town.[51]

Although each diocese has local power, SDF resources are set aside to sponsor new initiatives and enable the Church to have control over areas where the Church's reach is very weak. All the bids are supposed to help whatever has been established to become self-sustaining. However, some resource churches have devastated other churches and sucked up the human resources from other congregations. In an email I received towards the end of writing this book, a local vicar told me that one resource church nearby had a history of relationship destruction with other churches into whose areas of mission they have tried to plant.

'Worship first' journey

Mike Moynagh suggests that new ecclesial communities develop in a number of ways. The model dominating resource churches is what Moynagh calls the 'worship first' journey or approach and starts with a team of 20–40 sent by a larger church like Holy Trinity Brompton. Public worship is launched in vacant premises or a church building threatened with closure, and the new congregation can scale up quickly. It can be fruitful among people who are hanging on to the Church by the tips of their fingernails. But Moynagh points out that this model is often ill-suited to a post-Christian society where many will be unwilling or unable to take the long leap into church life.[52]

The resource church model often starts from a 'worship first' principle. In missional terms it's essentially attractional – that is, like a shop window selling its wares, or something rooted in a 'build it and they will come' philosophy. Many resource churches have upfront funding from SDF of sometimes several million. Start with a vicar, a curate, a worship leader, an operations manager and a refurbished church – and boom, lift off. A fully fledged church likely to attract young adults and students is up and running in a short space of time. Good examples of this are Gas Street in Birmingham and St Matts in Exeter.[53]

In their worst incarnations these revitalizations rooted in the resource church model bring a tyranny of change that does not bode well for the future Church. Alicia Crosby suggests that this 'worship first' journey or traditional model can actually be seen as a form of spiritual gentrification. She says:

It is not funny when people with means and privilege enter into a space and exert their will over that of the people who are long time residents. It is not funny when individuals who are planting these churches are allocated resources that spiritual communities who have been in solidarity and relationship with residents do not receive. It is not funny to see that time and time again people with racial and economic privilege exercise the hubris to start something outside of the places that they've called home just because they want to and they can.[54]

These criticisms shouldn't be brushed aside. However, in research from The Centre for Theology & Community, Thorlby[55] reflects more graciously on the revitalization of five churches in east London. It is 'the first fully-researched and published account of the church planting that has been undertaken in east London through the Holy Trinity Brompton (HTB) Network.'[56] This paints, and perhaps rightly so, a positive portrait of the revitalization narrative. The growth in a relatively short period of time in the five parishes was significant: 'Attendance of adults and children across the five churches has grown from 72 before the planting process to nearly 750.'[57] One in five are either returning to church or completely new to church. Some 80 per cent are people who have moved into the church as part of the revitalization planting team. There is much to celebrate but challenges remain.

With financial incentives from the HTB network, this revitalization model has been rolled out as the framework of choice
for planting, and makes new resource churches favourable for
bishops to consider in hard-pressed dioceses. In some instances,
the introduction of a new resource church in a city comes as
a complete surprise to local clergy and ecumenical partners.
Consultation can be minimal. There is also some confusion
over what exactly a resource church is. Being designated as a
resource church and included on the list at the Church Revitalisation Trust is no guarantee that you buy into the model. A
curate friend of mine admitted that even the resource church
she helped to lead didn't know what it really meant.

But I don't want what I have written above to be another
contribution to the already fierce culture wars that are raging
in the Church of England at present. I have been pleased to
see that there are more churches being planted in places like
Rochdale and Sheffield, and more diversity in leadership both
in terms of gender and race, but there is no one solution to the
complex challenges of church in the future.

While resource churches are particularly popular in order
to release funding, seeing local-appropriate new contextual
churches grow can take a long time. Timeframes for planting
new communities that are really embedded into the community are slow, painful processes. First, the listening and
loving process should not be rushed. In fact, that process must
remain continuously. If we are to properly pay attention it will
take more than a few months, especially if we take Shier Jones
seriously when he says 'pioneering ministry cannot be done to
a community by someone who knows what they need. It can
only be done with a community by someone who shares their
need.'[58] Three years of funding may just about cover an initial
listening period, with perhaps the establishment of some key
relationships with local people and the beginning of a pattern
of meeting established, but whether that would look like a
mature expression of church that SDF managers and assessors
would be happy with is uncertain.

Time frames and time*full* mission – 'serving first' journey

I want to suggest that the timeframes for funding need to be longer. There need to be fluid, more nimble structures and the encouragement of bi-vocational leadership. In my work with CTE I meet with pioneers in many different locations serving a wide variety of contexts. Moynagh suggests that an alternative model for the birthing of new ecclesial communities – in contrast to the 'worship first' model – is the 'serving first' journey. A serving first journey is birthed in praying, listening, loving and serving. That is not to say that resource churches do not pray or serve or love – far from it. However, resource churches have a very clear idea of what they want to do, the stages that must be followed, and the ecclesial outcomes. A service first model should really be utterly open to what the Spirit may birth in and through and with the community. Therefore, these first stages of the journey in post-Christendom soil will have the potential to be very slow. In the stories below the praying, listening, loving and serving are all deep parts of growing trust.

Hilary and Tom moved to a coastal town in the South West supported by two missional agencies. Having been in place for three years they were just beginning to see doors open to serve the community, many of whom were marginalized through winter poverty as the summer season was short because of the pandemic in 2020. Hilary told me that in their previous post they had spent 16 years on a large outer housing estate, and it took the first 10 years just to build trust. Funding that is withdrawn after three or five years fails to understand how long it really takes to establish deep incarnational presence. Funding should be more flexible. A half-time funding post for 10 years could allow a pioneer the opportunity to find work in the community. Hilary said she was constantly surprised how roles came up within a community that complemented the pioneering role she felt called to do. She has worked in cafés, run a playgroup, and worked for the local council. This allows both the institution and those working for it to acknowledge how often we are humbled by time rather than trying to live being harassed by time. As Hauerwas puts it, 'God *became* time with Christ, which means we have all the time in the world to do what is necessary.'[59]

Another example is Kevin and Lucy. They returned from 15 years of working alongside the Catholic Church in rural France. Full of enthusiasm, wisdom and experience of building deep and lasting relationships in a small village in the Burgundy region, they joined a large diocese in central England to pioneer a fresh expression of church. Funding came from the local parish which was keen to start something new, and was matched by the diocesan growth fund. Within three years they had gathered a community of people who were meeting together on a regular basis and exploring faith. However, funding to continue with the work was denied when the parish council decided it would be better to ring fence the remaining funds they had towards repairing the roof. Neither Kevin nor Lucy were invited to share the story of their work at the parish council nor how they hoped it would grow. In the end the person in charge of flowers had the deciding vote on whether to deny any further funding. She had never met Kevin or Lucy and had no previous knowledge of the project.

If the mission of the Church is simply to be about joining in with *missio Dei* perhaps the notion of being humbled by time would act as an antidote to the tyranny of the urgent. Perhaps it can dissolve our existential anxiety about future church? If God is slow and slow is valued, our frenzied time-deprived drives for efficiency will be knocked down like the straw figures they really are. John Swinton has written, 'if we orientate ourselves within the slow and powerful rhythms of God, we find time to pay the right kind of attention to the world'.[60] That cracking open, and slowing down, of time can lead us to paying the right type of attention in various situations. One of the services in the Greek Orthodox Church called 'The Service of the Hours' instructs the priest to sing the line 'be attentive' before the reading of the Gospel. It is paying attention to the small and barely noticeable. Paying attention to being people over the numbers. Remembering that, as Koyama says, 'hope is not a time-story. It is a love-story.'[61]

Measuring for joy

But this is not just a question about timescales and time*full*ness. It also asks questions about what we are looking for in our measures of success and growth. Recent work by Theos and the Church Urban Fund could be very helpful in reassessing some of the typical metrics used to measure success. In her comprehensive study *Growing Good: Growth, Social Action and Discipleship in the Church of England*, Hannah Rich notes that 'it is the language or approach to numerical growth and its measurement that some feel uncomfortable with, not that they think it is actively a bad thing to want to see the church grow'.[62] Rich writes:

> In terms of numerical growth, it is important not only that it is measured, but also what is measured and how it is done. The Church of England defines and measures church growth in terms of parish-level trends over a ten-year period. The experience of what church growth 'feels like' can sometimes be at odds with the quantitative classifications.[63]

Church growth that is singularly focused on measurements and metrics and bums on seats on Sundays becomes an ideological trope that fails to assess how the Church may be growing in other ways and at other points. Lesslie Newbigin has pointed out that this growth narrative has been enshrined in capitalist culture since the Scottish philosopher Adam Smith wrote *The Wealth of Nations* in 1776, and posited the idea of exponential growth at which no limits can be set. But growth for growth's sake is the ideology of the cancer cell.[64] We may rejoice in growth, but we may not worship it.

A case in point can be seen in research I undertook from 2016 to 2019 in Cape Town.[65] The church's Sunday morning congregations were quite small. One Book of Common Prayer service attracted between 5 and 10 people and the main Sunday service hovered around the 40 to 50 mark. However, the midweek (Thursday) Community Supper saw anywhere from 80 to 120 people gather to pray, reflect and eat a meal together. Every other week about 20 to 30 people would stay for an informal Eucharist led by an ordained minister. Numbers of those attending were recorded every week but, given the nature of the gathering, it was not officially recognized or accepted by the diocesan bishop at the time, who was not encouraging of forms of church that didn't look like he thought they should. Yet there was much to celebrate and rejoice over among the motley crew of 'on the road' disciples. There were certainly stories of transformation, people journeying towards Jesus, but often in haphazard ways.

At the Community Supper there were a number of people who had made journeys away from the addiction to drugs and alcohol. Others had found somewhere safe to live after a considerable period (in some cases generations) of being on the streets. Others had been helped in securing an identity document (vital for doing many things in South Africa). Still others had committed to studying the Bible with leaders of the community. These are stories of slow but significant transformation that cannot simply be captured in the services register. As Pierre Teilhard de Chardin reminds us in his poem 'Patient Trust': 'Above all, trust in the slow work of God. We are quite naturally impatient in everything to reach the end without delay.'[66]

Hannah Rich tells other stories of growth that may be seen as incremental transformation, of lives changed on a journey towards Jesus without it being an attendance statistic. In a particular case study one man who had come into regular contact with the church through an outreach project 'no longer found himself in situations of running away from the police'. Another very openly said:

When I first came here, I was bad-tempered and I kept getting wound up. It just didn't end well at all. Doors got broken. Hands got broken. I'd say I was a horrible person. I don't want to swear on your recording, but I was an arsehole. I had the biggest ego and I walked in thinking I was better than everyone else. Now I just think we're all humans loved by God.[67]

In both these cases neither person had made a profession of faith, nor were they regular attenders of a Sunday service; therefore they might not be counted as disciples but clearly had experienced some kind of transformation and were journeying towards Jesus. This kind of curious counting guards against commodifying people or turning them into numbers. A recent conversation with a researcher priest suggested that a way of measuring success in the first year for a team on a new housing estate was counting the number of people who smiled and waved at the core team. We need an urgent debate about creative and curious ways to measure growing things. Heather Cracknell's 'Fruitfulness Framework'[68] for fresh expressions in the Church of England has been a really helpful step in the right direction as the Church begins to think about measuring for joy.

Pace and pilgrimage

What does all this mean for the Church as it navigates its way into the future? If living more timefully and operating from a position of being humbled by time is central, we will need to replace the three-year SDF bid with the three-mile-an-hour God setting the pace. There are a variety of models and ways of seeing the Church flourish but we do need to be more mindful of the expectations around how things will grow and flourish and the sometimes (blunt) instruments we use to determine them.

Perhaps the idea of walking should become more significant in our mission and ministry journeys? When we see ourselves as pilgrims on a journey that is longer than we care to admit, or imagine, we have to be aware of our pace. Koyama says, 'when we walk, we see, we feel, smell and hear so many interesting things. We are not shut up. We are not rushing at fifty miles an hour. Our pace is three miles an hour on our own feet.'[69]

When we (literally) walk our neighbourhood we are embodying a holy rhythm. As we take time to discover where God is already at work, we honour the community we enter. The authors of the 2021 'Politics of Grace and Place' letter have reminded us that in many instances churches have fallen out of relationship with the ground they rest in and on. Re-establishing that, they say, 'is slow but holy work, requiring patient attention to our immediate context and prioritising time spent with neighbours – more accidental and in situ conversations than meetings with agenda. It means sharing meals, walking together, meeting for coffee, and hearing each other's woes.'[70] It means slowing down. It means following the three-mile-an-hour God. It means living in what Koyama called secret strength where we are restful yet full of actions.[71] There, I believe, is the future sustenance for the Church.

Notes

1 K. Koyama, 1979, *Three Mile an Hour God*, London: SCM Press, p. viiii.

2 R. Solnit, 2002, *Wanderlust: A History of Walking*, London: Granta, p. 5.

3 K. Koyama, 1979, *50 Meditations*, Maryknoll, NY: Orbis Books, p. 149.

4 F. Gros (translated J. Howe), 2015, *A Philosophy of Walking*, London: Verso Books, p. 6.

5 Ecclesiastes 3.11.

6 H. Garceau, 2014, 'The Sanctification of Time and the Liturgy of Hours', *Thomas Aquinas College*, https://thomasaquinas.edu/news/fr-hildebrand-sanctification-time-and-liturgy-hours, accessed 23.3.2022.

7 J. Swinton, 2017, *Becoming Friends of Time: Disability, Timefulness and Gentle Discipleship*, London: SCM Press, p. 23.

8 S. Johnson, 2015, *How We Got to Now: Six Innovations that Made the Modern World*, London: Penguin, p. 136.

9 Johnson, *How We Got to Now*, p. 135.

10 Johnson, *How We Got to Now*, p. 153.

11 J. Ritzer, 1998, *The McDonaldization Thesis*, London: Sage.

12 J. Begbie. 2000, *Theology, Music and Time*, Cambridge: Cambridge University Press, p. 73.

13 C. Honoré, 2004, *In Praise of Slow*, London: Orion Publishing, p. 20.

14 F. T. Marinetti, 1909, 'The Futurist Manifesto', *Bactra*, https://bactra.org/T4PM/futurist-manifesto.html, accessed 23.3.2022. Note: Text of translation taken from James Joll, 2020, *Three Intellectuals in Politics: Blum Rathenau and Marinetti*, Lexington, MA: Plunkett Lake Press.

15 L. Bicker, '"I thought maybe I would die": S Korea's delivery drivers demand change', *BBC News*, 3 November, https://www.bbc.co.uk/news/world-asia-54775719, accessed 23.3.2022.

16 Koyama, *Three Mile an Hour God*, p. 15.

17 Begbie, *Theology, Music and Time*, p. 71.

18 Swinton, *Becoming Friends of Time*, p. 58.

19 Augustine, *Confessions*, Book XI, p. 14.

20 Augustine, *Confessions*, Book XI, p. 12.

21 Garceau, 'The Sanctification of Time and the Liturgy of Hours'.

22 Swinton, *Becoming Friends of Time*, p. 27.

23 Swinton, *Becoming Friends of Time*, p. 25.

24 G. Jantzen, 1983, 'Time and Timelessness' in A. Richardson and J. Bowden (eds), *A New Dictionary of Christian Theology*, London: SCM Press, p. 574.

25 P. Virilio, 1977, *Speed and Politics: An Essay on Dromology*, New York: Semiotext(e).

26 K. Koyama, 1974, *Waterbuffalo Theology*, Maryknoll, NY: Orbis Books, p. 12.

27 Mark 1.15.

28 Koyama, *Three Mile an Hour God*, p. 109.

29 Koyama, *Three Mile an Hour God*, p. 6.

30 It's worth remembering that Koyama was writing in an era when technology was in its infancy.

31 Acts 8.39.

32 Koyama, *Three Mile an Hour God*, p. 13.

33 Koyama, *Three Mile an Hour God*, p. 15.

34 Koyama, *Three Mile an Hour God*, p. 7.

35 K. Koyama, 1975, '"Not by Bread alone ..." How Does Jesus Free and Unite Us?', *The Ecumenical Review* 24(3), p. 201.

36 Koyama, '"Not by Bread alone ..."', p. 203.

37 K. Koyama, 1977, *No Handle on the Cross: An Asian Meditation on the Crucified Mind*, London: SCM Press, p. 5.

38 Alan Roxburgh, 'Our collective handwringing', *Alan Roxburgh*, https://alanroxburgh.com/2019/11/our-collective-handwringing/, accessed 23.3.2022.

39 General Synod, 1976, 'In Each Generation', *Church of England*, https://www.churchofengland.org/sites/default/files/2017-11/gs%20 1976%20-%20a%20note%20from%20the%20archbishops%20 giving%20an%20overview%20of%20the%20task%20groups.pdf, accessed 23.3.2022.

40 General Synod, 1978, 'Report of the Task Force on Resourcing the Future of the Church of England', *Church of England*, https:// www.churchofengland.org/sites/default/files/2017-11/gs%201978%20 -%20resourcing%20the%20future%20task%20group%20report.pdf, accessed 23.3.2022.

41 'Report of the Task Force on Resourcing the Church of England', p. 1.

42 Church Times, 2015, 'Use central funds to subsidise growth, not decline, says task group', *Church Times*, 16 January, https://www. churchtimes.co.uk/articles/2015/16-january/news/uk/use-central-funds- to-subsidise-growth-not-decline-says-task-group, accessed 23.3.2022.

43 Church of England, 'Strategic Development Funding', *Church of England*, https://www.churchofengland.org/about/renewal-reform/ funding-mission-and-growth/strategic-development-funding, accessed 23.3.2022.

44 Renewal and Reform, 'Strategic Development Funding Application Process', *Church of England*, https://www.churchofengland.org/ sites/default/files/2019-11/SDF%20QA%20briefing%20-%20July %202019_4.pdf, p. 4, accessed 23.3.2022.

45 M. Davies, 2019, 'Revitalising mission – but at what cost?', *Church Times*, https://www.churchtimes.co.uk/articles/2019/22-nov ember/features/features/revitalising-mission-but-at-what-cost, accessed 23.3.2022.

46 B. Aldous, 2020, 'Pasties, Pirates and Practical Theology: Taking Cornish Context and Culture Seriously when Utilising the Resource Church Model', *Rural Theology Journal* 18(2), pp. 2–12.

47 M. Moynagh, 2017, *Church in Life: Innovation, Mission and Ecclesiology*, London: SCM Press.

48 Names have been anonymized throughout this chapter.

49 M. A. Kool, 2016, 'A Missiologist's Look at the Future: A Missiological Manifesto for the 21st Century' in C. Constantineanu, M. V. Măcelaru, A. M. Kool and M. Himcinschi (eds), *Mission in Central and Eastern Europe: Realities, Perspectives, Trends*, Oxford: Regnum, p. 695.

50 Church Revitalisation Trust, 'What we do', *CRT*, https://crtrust. org/work.

51 R. Thorpe, 2020, 'City Centre Resource Churches: Training to Enable Church Planting', unpublished DMin thesis, Ashbury Theological Seminary.

52 Moynagh, *Church in Life*, pp. 39–40.

53 See https://gasstreet.church/ and https://www.stmattsexeter.org.

54 A. T. Crosby, 2021, 'But What Is Church Planting, If Not Spiritual Gentrification Persevering?', *Alicia T. Crosby*, 4 March, https://www.aliciatcrosby.com/blog/2021/3/4/but-what-is-church-planting-if-not-spiritual-gentrification-persevering, accessed 23.3.2022.

55 T. Thorlby, 2016, 'Love, Sweat and Tears. Church planting in east London', London: The Centre for Theology and Community, https://www.theology-centre.org.uk/wp-content/uploads/2013/04/ChurchPlanting_Final_online.pdf, accessed 23.3.2022.

56 Thorlby, 'Love, Sweat and Tears', p. i.

57 Thorlby, 'Love, Sweat and Tears', p. iii.

58 A. Shier Jones, 2009, *Pioneer Ministry and Fresh Expression of Church*, London: SPCK, p. 163.

59 A. Klager, 2014, 'The vulnerability that makes peace possible: An interview with Stanley Hauerwas', *Huffpost*, 14 July, https://www.huffpost.com/entry/the-vulnerability-that-ma_b_5579366, accessed 4.2.2021.

60 Swinton, *Becoming Friends of Time*, p. 208.

61 K. Koyama, 1998, 'Together on the Way: 2.4. Rejoice in Hope', *World Council of Churches*, 8th Assembly, 3–14 December, Harare, Zimbabwe, https://www.oikoumene.org/resources/documents/together-on-the-way-24-rejoice-in-hope, accessed 23.3.2022.

62 H. Rich, 2020, *Growing Good: Growth, Social Action and Discipleship in the Church of England*, https://www.theosthinktank.co.uk/cmsfiles/GRACE-CUF-v10-combined.pdf, accessed 23.11.2020, p. 28.

63 Rich, *Growing Good*, p. 29.

64 L. Newbigin, 1986, *Foolishness to the Greeks*, London: SPCK, p. 114.

65 Part of this story is captured in B. Aldous, I. Dunmore and M. Seevaratnam, 2021, *Intercultural Church: Shared Learning from New Communities*, Cambridge: Grove Books. B. Aldous, 2019, '"How Can We Sing When We're in a Strange Land?" Practical Theology as Performance and Improvisation in a Post-colonial Context', *Journal of Theology for Southern Africa* 165, pp. 24–49.

66 P. Teilhard de Chardin, 1993, 'Patient Trust' in M. Harter (ed), *Hearts on Fire: Praying with the Jesuits*, Chicago, IL: Loyola Press, p. 102.

67 Rich, *Growing Good*, p. 99.

68 Heather Cracknell, https://www.churchofengland.org/about/evangelism-and-discipleship/mission-network-news/fruitfulness-framework-what-we-measure-2.

69 Koyama, *50 Meditations*, p. 149.

70 A. Rumsey, J. Sinclair et al. 2021, 'The Politics of Grace and Place: A Letter to the local Church', *Journal of Missional Practice* (Winter), https://journalofmissionalpractice.com/grace-and-place/, accessed 19.3.2021, p. 2.

71 Koyama, *Three Mile an Hour God*, p. 80.

3

Seeing:
Notes in the Margins

Introduction

Walking slowly between villages, never seeming to be in a hurry, Jesus reached out to, and moved towards, those on the periphery. He insisted on seeing the children who were being kept from him on the margins of the masses. Jesus made a fuss until the woman who had been healed of her bleeding by touching his cloak had revealed herself in the crowd. He went out of his way to honour a divine appointment with the Samaritan woman by the well. He incurred the wrath of a town by noticing Zacchaeus up a tree and inviting himself over for a meal. He constantly noted those on the margins. In fact, Jesus is the God of the marginalized, the overlooked and unnoticed.

Jesus embodied the action of God, always moving from the centre to the periphery, always acting as a good neighbour, demonstrating the true hospitality of God. In Luke's Gospel Jesus is seen time and again positioning himself alongside those considered to be the damned or despised by society: the demonized, the oppressed, the tax frauds, the prostitutes, the deaf, dumb, lame, various categories of outcast, foreigners, the list goes on. Jesus, who was the human being most profoundly available to, and aware of, the Holy Spirit was committed to doing only what he saw his Father doing. Jesus' nourishment came through that way of being,[1] continually noticing and loving those at the edges and inviting them towards the centre.

If you have ever lived for a number of years outside the country of your birth, you might have experienced something of the discombobulation felt on returning 'home'. It's a common problem for many third culture children, and increasingly a normal experience for many in our globalized societies. The place you thought you knew has changed in the intervening years that you have been away, and so have you. When I returned from 15 years of living in South Africa and Cambodia, I found it difficult to feel I was home. Things looked familiar yet people and places felt alien to me. I wear a pin badge on the lapel of my winter coat. It's made up of three flags: Cambodia, South Africa and Cornwall. I sometimes say I have three hearts. I'm Cornish by birth, I have a South African green ID book, and I have old passports full of Cambodian visas. My life has been profoundly shaped by other places, and the people of those places. In a way we are all called to live in the tension of our identity in Jesus Christ and our national identity, but there have been times when we have clung to our national identities in ways that can be harmful to others.

Over the past four or so years of returning to the UK I've noticed that I often find more relational resonance with people who have come to this country to make it their home, who are resident aliens, for want of a better phrase. Whether getting to know a Greek Orthodox priest and enjoying the hospitality of good Greek revani and coffee, eating a meal with a new Indian friend, or reflecting on what mission in the UK might look like with a Malawian theologian, I have felt a sense of connection with those who occupy the margins, even if only partially. The British Christian landscape has been immensely enriched over the last half a century by the gift of Christians from across the globe, whether from Africa, Asia, South America, the Middle East or the edges of Europe. Tragically, we have often failed to notice this gift in our midst or even to tolerate it. History is replete with examples of how those from the Windrush generation came to join our historic denominations but often were made to feel less than welcome. Yet as I watched the Tokyo Olympics in the summer of 2021, I was reminded again and again that a number of Team GB's medals were a direct result of the gift of migration. I believe our lives, heart and futures are so intertwined with our openness to the gift of our majority world brothers and sisters that shunning, rejecting and dismissing them will ultimately not only impoverish us, but actually be the death of us.

When I was a vicar in Cape Town I was invited (along with other clergy in the diocese) to Bishopscourt to have tea on an annual basis with Archbishop Thabo Makgoba. Standing in a large circle in one of the anterooms of the residence, the archbishop would look round the circle and welcome us with the IsiZulu greeting of *sawubona*. *Sawubona* is the greeting used when you welcome anyone into your home or are passing a friend on the street. It's much more than our 'hello'. Literally translated it means 'we see you'. It's a profound acknowledgement of the other. Not simply I notice you, but I see you, I recognize you, you are valued, you are welcome.

In this chapter I want to consider the Church and its mission legacy and how often that has been deeply connected to an appalling record of imperialistic violence and empire building. I ask how Koyama's concepts of 'neighbourology' and hospitality to strangers could be useful starting points for undoing some of that and might enable us to 'see' ourselves and others better. I consider the 'gift' of migration into the UK of Christians from across the globe as a way of both challenging and renewing our lives together. Neighbourology (a typical Koyama neologism) and hospitality towards strangers act as a way of framing a conversation about seeing those at the edges or in the margins, and embracing the gift they are to us. By exploring these themes, I hope they open up another route (by re-examining our roots) for the Church to take more seriously the gift of migration to the UK over the past 60 years or so. I share two stories of Christians who have made their home in the UK and their experiences.

Koyama's 'bombing'

Not long after his retirement from formal teaching at Union Theological Seminary in New York, Koyama, in a reflection on his pilgrimage in mission, wrote that it was only later in his life that he came to understand something of the suffering of black and Jewish people. It's worth remembering that Koyama's experience of the bombing and destruction of Tokyo as a teenager had already profoundly shaped his ideas around idolatry, power and violence. Koyama grew up in a homogeneous Japan with a zealous nationalism, yet up until the late 1970s his experience had largely been in East Asia and New Zealand (although he did do his doctoral work in the USA). His move to New York in 1980 was a second 'bombing':

> I experienced a 'bombing' quite different from that I had known during the wartime of my youth. There, for the first time, I encountered the Jewish and black peoples. New York abruptly forced me to respond theologically to the fact of enormous violence suffered by these two peoples. My concept of theology, which is ecumenical by nature, did not allow me the excuse that I come from a land in which these two peoples had no historical connections. I sensed that my identity would be directly threatened if I did not come to terms with the twofold encounter.[2]

Koyama reflected that 'these two peoples are a symbol representing millions of other people who have suffered violence and perished in the course of human history. Their very presence in our midst raises the ultimate question of violence in human civilization.' While Koyama had begun to develop the idea of neighbourology during his time in Chiang Mai in the 1960s, his move to New York, this 'bombing', was in some sense a second conversion.

'Neighbourology'

Victoria Lee Erickson says that Koyama understood what good neighbouring is all about: 'By listening to the stories of our neighbours and participating in the stories themselves, we achieve community. But building community takes time based not on efficient confrontation but on inefficient patience.'[3]

This idea of 'neighbourology' is rooted in the greatest two commandments: to love the Lord your God with all our heart, mind and soul and to love our neighbour as ourselves. Koyama says that good theology is talk that takes one's neighbour seriously. Jesus was, after all, suggests Koyama, a 'neighbour-logical' man.[4] He recounts a story of his attempts to share the gospel with an elderly sick Thai woman who was less than impressed with the fact that he could not speak her local northern dialect. Koyama points out that in the interaction the woman 'was annoyed at me for looking at her *in my own terms*. She felt that she was only an object of my religious conquest. I had a message for her, but I did not think that she had a message for me. She noticed this imperialistic one-sidedness.'[5] Our sense of the presence of God will be distorted if we fail to see God's reality in terms of our neighbour's reality. Theology for Koyama had become too caught up with questions that are dislocated from the concrete reality of people and their experiences in the world. When people become our 'projects' or part of our 'religious conquest' we are in trouble, and while almost no one would, I suspect, consciously see others as 'project material', deeper reflection on how we engage or interact with them may reveal something quite different.

When I first arrived at the church in Cape Town I preached a series of sermons entitled 'Mission as …' (an idea I stole from David Bosch). At the end of the service one morning as people lined up at the door to shake my hand or hug me, one woman, looking aghast, said to me, 'I've made Barry a project my entire life!' Barry, her alcoholic husband, with whom she had a complex and deteriorating relationship, had made little movement, from her perspective, towards Jesus. Carol knew her 'projecting' of Barry was in no way helping. Project and object being so interlinked as to be indistinguishable from each other, Carol began to think about how she might better reveal Jesus to Barry.

When people defy our simplistic categorization of them, we are guilty of depersonalizing and not taking seriously what Sartre understood to be the 'monstrous freedom' of all human beings. Genuine neighbourology allows us to be thwarted, encountered, shaped, sent off course and trans- formed by others. In the next chapter I explore this in more detail, but Koyama believed that the objectification of human beings for the purposes of an evangelism stratagem was ulti- mately dehumanizing. Koyama often reflected upon the church growth movement's obsession with numbers and the commod- ification of people as 'number': 'I am convinced somewhere in the depth of quality of "being human" that I, the human being, am of greater value than even two billion pounds. The idea of two billion people comes to me in a completely different way. Immediately I sense I cannot tame them, I cannot control them, I cannot possess them.' There is 'a sacred dimension in man [and woman] which defies and rejects being numbered'.[6] To practise neighbourology, then, is to be profoundly aware of the *imago Dei* in each man, woman and child we come into contact and relationship with.

Hospitality towards strangers

Interconnected with this is Koyama's exploration of hospital- ity towards strangers. He was bold enough to say, 'Christian theology will remain meaningful only as long as it takes the stranger seriously'[7] and that the ancient vision of 'extending hospitality of strangers' is the beginning of mission.[8]

Koyama wondered if many of us feel distaste when we hear English spoken with an accent?[9] Or if we can instead act in wonder that someone is bravely communicating in perhaps their second or third or fourth language? Might we then be fascinated when we hear English spoken with an accent? Fascinated by the story that person may embody? Recognizing, of course, that in the UK we have a rich tapestry of 'accents', there can be suspicion when the 'accent' is not regional (for example, someone from Yorkshire or Cornwall) but is noticeably 'foreign'.

Koyama says that extending hospitality to strangers happens by the mercies of God and this only occurs when our lives become a 'living sacrifice' as a part of spiritual worship.[10] Koyama is once again linking missiology with doxology. We are called then to extend hospitality to strangers because Jesus comes to us as a stranger (Matthew 25.35). We are called to extend hospitality to strangers because, as Koyama reminds us, 'Christ was crucified because he extended hospitality to strangers so completely.'[11] The result of offering hospitality to strangers could result in you being killed – it's called martyrdom.

In the Old Testament the people of Israel were profoundly shaped by the root experience of the exodus and the fact that they were rejected and cast out by Pharaoh and the Egyptians. As a result, 'Israel's contemplation on their relationship with the stranger offers us a relevant evangelical counsel. It is the ancient vision of "extending hospitality to strangers".'[12]

I wonder if we are in need of an experience of a 'bombing' that might act as a kind of conversion point – a circumcision of the heart, scales falling from our eyes into seeing more deeply?

How are we responding to the growing anxiety that has surfaced as a result of the problems of immigration, living with the 'other', identity politics, the Black Lives Matter (BLM) movement, the Brexit fallout and the crisis of the coronavirus pandemic and its aftermath? I suggest that there may be a flourishing through the cracks of parochialism and prejudice, but not necessarily from the centre or the national structures of any church but instead by hearing the stories of those who have come to make their home in our midst and the transformational effect it can have. I share the stories of Rita (Lithuania) and Harvey (Malawi) as encouragement. The chapter closes with some reflections on future church as intercultural church.

Who is at your table?

Who is at your table is an important metaphorical and literal question we should be posing at the personal, local and national institutional level. Let me share two stories of eating a meal around a table that stand out in my mind as great occasions – but for completely different reasons.

The first meal took place in lavish surroundings: a private dining room of Hartford House in the KwaZulu-Natal Midlands in South Africa. It's one of those restaurants you only get to go to once in a lifetime (unless you have the wallet). Everything about it screamed exclusive. There were only four or five tables and probably a maximum of 15 guests present. Each course had been thought about in exquisite detail. A soup that included pouring in little pods which exploded (delightfully) in our mouths, all the way to a finale of handmade petits fours infused with tobacco and were such a surprise we laughed out loud. Eating the meal with my wife, my sister and her husband – a night away from the children – made it extra special. But it was, in no way, inclusive.

The second meal was quite the opposite. In my early days at St John's Wynberg in Cape Town, I was keen to help the congregation I led to think about how they might connect with the local community in more intentional ways. Together with other church leaders in the area (most notably the Methodists, Vineyard, Presbyterians and a local charismatic fellowship), we decided to try and feast together on the basis of bringing enough food for ourselves and another guest. We met in the local park which in some ways acted as a buffer between the wealthy and slightly exclusive Little Chelsea area and the main road usually bustling with the life of people from not only Cape Town, but often across the whole continent. For some in the congregation this was an exciting opportunity to be seized and enjoyed. For others it was rife with security risks and potential pandemonium should our feast be overrun with homeless people seeking to steal all the food. (I kid you not!) The reality was much less exciting but more profound. Parading down to Maynardville Park after church with picnics overflowing and congregating with others from churches in the area was in fact joyful. We pooled all our food and spread it out on large tables, prayed, and invited people to come and eat. Some church members set up a couch offering anyone who wanted it an opportunity to share in prayer. Within 10–15 minutes the word had spread around the local homeless community and people lined up for a plate of food. But the word also got out to the local police station just across the road and to security guards. People who just happened to be taking a Sunday stroll were urged to join us. Finally, a small congregation of Zimbabweans who met for fellowship in a nearby upper room on the main street were walking past and joined us. I have no idea how many people ate or the types of conversations and prayer that took place, but I remember thinking at one point as I watched everything unfolding that this (however imperfectly) embodied something of a heavenly banquet that will take place when God comes and makes God's home in our midst (Luke 14.12–14). The gathering was certainly made up of many people who were not usually made welcome for a number of reasons. We were attempting to practise hospitality towards strangers.

Mission history, imperialism and violence

We know that mission history has not always embodied hospitality towards the marginalized and overlooked – that is, the stranger. Yet Koyama says mission is in essence extending hospitality to strangers.[13] I don't want to disparage all the good that has been done in the name of Christian mission over the centuries. There were, and are, women and men who sacrificed their lives in humility and with gentleness to share the story of Jesus in conditions of great challenge. Those should be honoured. One such example is Henry Townsend, a CMS missionary and the first alongside Samuel Ajayi Crowther in working with the Yoruba people of Nigeria. Townsend often spoke on behalf of the Yoruba people to the British authorities.

But we should not imagine there were only a handful of instances of violence and subjugation over the past centuries. I don't say this to disparage or mock what happened in the past but to bring us to a point of honest – perhaps painful – reflection, contrition and sober judgement about missionary imperialism and the violence, physical, social and spiritual, connected to it. The discovery of an estimated 751 unmarked graves in June 2021 at the site of the former Marieval residential school in Saskatchewan in Canada tells a horrifying story. Operated by the Roman Catholic Church from 1899 to the 1980s it is an appalling reminder of the way the Church was instrumental in systemic racism, and the barbaric treatment of indigenous peoples.[14]

There isn't space in this book to write about all the various connections between mission, imperialism and colonialism in all its forms. But, to be quite clear, colonialism was not a benign entity. Kenyan writer Yvonne Adhiambo Owuor's visceral outline sets the scene:

> What people call 'the age of colonialism' ought to be addressed by its rightful moniker, 'the age of atrocity,' for its egregious will to violence, its slaughter of humans worldwide, for offenses against nature, for the frenzied, inhuman, and obscene worship of the golden calf. With very few exceptions, colonial hoards behaved like beasts. No, beasts act with greater integrity; they acted like demons, like people possessed by a void.[15]

Koyama argued consistently in his writings that Christianity gave the impression it was ahistorical. 'I do not think Christianity in Asia for the last four hundred years has really listened to the people. It has ignored people. It has ignored the spirituality of people. It has ignored people's deep aspiration and frustration.'[16] Subsequently, a theology that is *not* rooted in the aspirations and frustrations of the people becomes a docetic theology.[17] Centuries of not only ignoring the hopes, joys, anxieties and gifts of people, but instead destroying them, continues to be a haunting legacy. Koyama says this is the posture of the crusading mind rather than the crucified mind. 'The church remains apostolic as long as the crucified mind stands in its heart and cries to the crucified Lord.'[18] And Irvin writes: 'His experience of living through the destruction of Tokyo and the surrender of the emperor led Koyama to be not only a theologian of suffering and repentance, but also a theologian of empire'.[19]

But it was more than not listening. In the Southern African context historian Greg Cuthbertson paints a picture difficult for some of us to acknowledge around the relationship between mission and violence. As a historian he reveals that an overwhelming portion of Christian missionaries believed that 'the British Empire was the greatest force for good in a world ripe for Christianity'.[20] Cuthbertson says this is seen in the way in which missionaries were involved in colonial warfare in the late nineteenth century. Missionaries were deeply engaged in the arms trade in the Cape Colony – and actively encouraged it in the middle of the nineteenth century where violence escalated. They were so captivated by imperialist ideology that it became seen as a valuable source of military intelligence. British missionaries almost without exception supported the British cause during the South African war in 1899–1902 because of their preoccupation with English supremacy.

Again, reflecting on the Southern African context, Harvey Kwiyani has written soberingly about the kind of deformed relationships the Christian mission enterprise had with its subjects. Kwiyani says that the imperialist attitudes that were prevalent in the nineteenth century continue to dominate the global scene through white supremacism. 'It is hard to imagine world Christianity without white supremacy. The folly of this imperial Christianity that wants to evangelise the marginalised and yet keep them oppressed and confined to the margins as second-class Christians is beyond comprehension.'[21] But for Kwiyani, and his identification as a recovering missiologist, the narrative is deeply rooted in his own family history. Kwiyani's great-great-great-grandfather, Ntimawanzako Nacho, was among the first Malawians to go to Scotland for theological training at Stewarts College in 1885 as part of Blantyre Mission's strategy for future leaders.[22] In 1861, Magomero became the site of the first mission station in central Africa. For Malawians this is the 'ground zero' site for mission and colonialism deeply woven together. By the time Nacho had returned after training, the land had become a colonial estate effectively stolen by David Livingstone's family. Kwiyani recounts the events of 24 January 1915:

> A local (American-trained) Baptist minister, John Chilembwe, had just led a somewhat successful uprising against the colonial government and to prove it, he preached his sermon with William Jervis Livingstone's severed head perched on a stick right next to the pulpit. The people celebrated – Chilembwe was their Moses, their messiah, the liberator.[23]

But it was not to last. It was Chilembwe's intention to strike a blow and die. As Maluleke questions:

> But what happens when the Africans do not surrender as easily and therefore do not exhibit the assumed weaknesses that should render them unfit to withstand European assault? What happens when they withstand the assault of the supposedly superior power of European powers?[24]

What happens is that the violence and subjugation on which the whole colonialist and imperialist project is built unleashes its fury. Those who attempted to resist were met with a violence that has been the hallmark of empire for several millennia.

While we may accept, however uncomfortable it feels, that there are parts of mission history based on ignoring, crushing and destroying local people's hopes and aspirations, what of today's situation and the overspill of the past into our contemporary narrative? We live in a world fraught with anxiety – the first part of the twenty-first century is arguably as volatile as the first decades of the twentieth. The post-colonial era that began in the post-war period and reached its height in the 1960s, and promised much in the potential self-realization of nations across Africa, Asia and South America, has not brought the longed-for transformation. Empire power still resides in the global north in a way that will bring even greater conflict and destruction if not tempered.

The age of anxiety

Antje Jackelén has commented that many countries of the world are drinking a dangerous cocktail of poisonous ingredients all beginning with P.[25] I use this as a way of framing what I call the age of anxiety while drawing on others to define and elucidate the English context more fully. Jackelén suggests that there are five Ps in her dangerous cocktail: polarization, populism, protectionism, post-truth and patriarchy.

First, polarization, says Jackelén, 'tears apart whole societies as well as smaller communities'.[26] It functions as a kind of binary. Old versus young, urban against rural, rich versus poor, etc. Polarization occurs when the narratives in the political arena, on social media and other networks, pit one set of people against another but this always refutes exceptions, is unable to deal with ambiguity, and often caricatures one group over and against another. Jackelén suggests that polarization often leads to populism.

Populism (or popularism) grows in the seedbed of polarization. 'Populists claim that they are the voice of the people – which is supposed to have just this one voice – that speaks out against the elites.'[27] This kind of populist narrative can be seen quite clearly among the far right in recent years in England. In a selection of academic papers produced as part of the government's commission on countering extremism,[28] Ben Lee writes that 'populist radical right parties have done well in elections across Europe and contributed to a wider narrative that liberal democratic norms are under threat'.[29] And that 'is

77

the belief that societies are split between virtuous masses of people and a narrow and corrupt elite'. That populism, Lee suggests, also hides a nativism and an authoritarianism that often successfully 'others' minorities whether defined racially, sexually or religiously.

Perhaps interlinked, and certainly related to this populism, is an idea in English minds of an exceptionalism since populism has a nativism about it. This myth has been powerfully exploited in the recent debates around having a no-deal Brexit. In its simplest form it is about manipulating our memory of the British empire and the fact that we once controlled a good third of the world. Justin Welby notes in his book *Reimagining Britain* that, like other nations, 'the UK is understood and understands itself, through stories it tells about itself ... but there are more nuanced histories asking awkward questions about popular ideas'.[30]

So, the argument goes, we were such a small nation yet capable of so much. Behind people's desire to leave the EU, as one blogger put it, 'the idea of plucky Britain going it alone in the world resonated particularly with elderly voters frustrated with the country's relative decline'.[31] Our exceptionalism myth continued to play itself out during the Covid-19 pandemic. We know best and our experts are the best was a narrative that cropped up time and again during the daily briefing from ministers. At times the government revealed (a softer, watered-down version of Trump) a suspicion and hostility towards co-ordinated international action at an institutional level. Harris says, 'In England in particular there is a strand of the national culture expressed by the mixture of hectoring optimism and insularity of the right wing press, and reducible to the idea that the supposed British way of doing anything is necessarily the best.'[32] Boris Johnson seemed to find it worryingly easy to use phrases like 'world beating' without examining how unhelpful that kind of language might actually be. Koyama links this idea when he writes 'exceptionalism, like dispensationalism and fundamentalism, arranges time and space for the exclusive salvation of a favoured group'.[33] Our exceptionalism is a myth and needs to be tempered with the attitude of Katherine Johnson, the African American NASA mathematician who died in February 2020. She said, 'My dad taught us, "You are as good as anybody in this town, but you're no better". I don't have a feeling of inferiority. Never had. I'm as good as anybody, but no better.'[34]

But underneath that notion of exceptionalism is the reality of the massive destructive force of the British empire. Collins says, 'Britain claimed for itself the status of the chosen nation and the mission of Britain was to witness to the purposes of God through British imperialism. The relationship between other nations and their indigenous populations were seen through the lens of Israel and their heathen neighbours.'[35] Our exceptionalism masks an appalling violence towards, and subjugation of, indigenous people in nearly every corner of the globe. It's not in the scope of this chapter to go into much detail but suffice to say more and more people are becoming aware of the dark and disturbing nature of the British empire and the continued fallout today. Dorling and Tomlinson suggest that the 'EU referendum showed up the last throws of the empire thinking working its way out of the British psyche'.[36] Empire ideology is founded on what all empires are founded on: violence, repression, gross injustice – the manipulation and subjugation of local peoples, cultures and resources. The British empire became 'addicted to receiving tribute'.[37] As the empire dissolved after World War Two the idea of our exceptionalism became a powerful myth to be weaponized. Others, like black liberationist theologian Anthony Reddie, argue that the notions of English manifest destiny, tied up with white nationalism and overt racism, have been an ongoing thread being weaved under the surface of Brexit.[38] Luke Bretherton has suggested it is simply a form of idolatry.[39]

Populism also feeds into Jackelén's third P: protectionism. This puts one's own group, nation or country, first, at the expense of common interests. 'America First' and Brexit are examples. Again, protectionism often functions in binary form, pitting itself against the forces of the globalized free trade that don't work in its favour but it is also intertwined with a nativism or nationalism that feeds it. Jackelén argues that 'in both cases we know that the campaigns were built on lies – on false facts, masked as "alternative facts" – which brings us to post-truth'.

A typical example of post-truth protectionism can be seen during the campaign on the referendum in 2016 to remain in Europe or not. The leave campaign famously used their Brexit bus to claim that £350 million was being sent to the EU every week which could be better spent on funding the NHS. This has largely been refuted and even Nigel Farage[40] has distanced himself from this claim, yet this powerful post-truth myth continues to hold much sway.[41]

Jackelén's final P is patriarchy, which she says is a 'disturbing background noise throughout history'.[42] The issue of patriarchy should not be dismissed as simply a 'final P'. All that is written above is predicated on the fact that most of those holding power, manipulating the masses and weaponizing myths of exceptionalism, are by and large white, Western, middle-aged men.

Migration, 'othering' and those at the margins – migrants as gifts for the whole church

I want to suggest that there may be an antidote to this dangerous cocktail of poisonous ingredients, which lies in how we protect, bless, care for and nurture those who often end up being spat at with this venom. Or how others are showing us how to do that.

Statistics suggest that hate crime has risen dramatically in England in recent years.[43] According to Home Office statistics there have been year on year increases in recorded hate crimes from roughly 40,000 in 2013 to well over 100,000 in 2019.[44] The majority of hate crimes were race hate crimes (about 79,000 or roughly 76 per cent of all recorded crimes), and migrants have often been on the receiving end of this bile.

Andrew Walls rightly reminds us that, 'migration seems to be basic to the human condition, for it has been repeated endlessly in human history'.[45] But is it not perhaps the most fundamental shaper of geopolitics in the twentieth century? Certainly, it was Koyama's observation back in the early 1980s: 'We are living again in a period when humanity is on the move. With and without the aid of modern technology millions are criss-crossing the globe.'[46]

What has often been ignored, or pushed aside, in the Brexit debacle is the fact that Britain itself is a hotchpotch of immigrants. Dorling and Tomlinson state, 'In the 5th and 6th centuries, following the fall of the Roman Empire, what we now call England was carved out by immigrant warlords to make tribal territories.'[47] English history is crisscrossed with immigrants.[48] Our bloodlines are mingled with those from across Europe, Africa and beyond. And yet in the twentieth century, starting with the 1905 Aliens Acts aimed at stopping the perceived flow of Eastern European Jews, we have found ways of limiting and opposing the giftings, skills and creativity of the migrants in our midst. By the mid-twentieth century with the dissolution of the empire and the loss of territory and power, 'Europe, imperial dreams faded, became absorbed in intra-European constructions, or in defining relations with the two new superpowers.'[49] Britain found that it had acquired a substantial new population from its former or residual colonies as an inescapable legacy of the colonial past.[50] The Windrush generation, who first arrived in June 1948, were not treated as the gift they should have been, neither were those of faith embraced by the national Church:

> Some of the Windrush generation found a warm welcome in parish churches, but many others experienced appalling racism. A paper to be submitted to the (general) synod includes an account from Doreen Browne, who arrived in the UK in 1956 aged 16. She described her mother being turned away on the steps of St Peter's church in Walworth, south London, 'due to the plain fact of the colour of her black skin'.[51]

Perhaps this is to be tempered by the 'dangerous memories' of Christianity's colonial heritage, although 'control of immigration has suddenly become a major issue in European politics. The developed world is faced with a paradox: it *needs* immigrants, but does not *want* them.'[52]

In recent years we have seen the flow of migrants from the outer parts of Europe. Ironically, our patron saint George of dragon-killing legend, was probably a migrant of Greek and Palestinian heritage. We may want to ask more searching questions about the gift of the immigrant community in an age of anxiety and how we might navigate the post-Brexit and post-coronavirus landscape. By sharing below the stories of Rita and Harvey I think it's possible to show that there are many voices we might listen to in order to learn what Christianity looks like today and it is 'necessary to integrate them into a wider concept and to describe the history of world Christianity as a history of multidirectional transregional and transcontinental interactions'.[53] But we need to guard against binary attitudes of Western and non-Western, or global south and global north. These typologies do not reflect the fractured, nuanced, multifaceted reality of experience of Christians historically or today.

Perhaps I am a 'prickly gift'? – Rita

I want to offer two recent examples of the gift of migrants in the English context. First, the work of the World Cafe in Gloucester, which before the pandemic was a thriving community. The World Cafe was initiated by Rita Rimkiene, a Lithuanian woman who also works for European Christian Mission and is now training to be a Baptist minister at Bristol Baptist College.[54] Rita came to faith after the collapse of the Berlin wall and, together with her husband, has served with European Christian Mission since 2010. Rita's attitude of hospitality is best summed up in her own words: 'God is a hospitable Creator, welcoming all into His world, the family enjoy welcoming people into their home. Here, the mundane conversations turn into prayer, discovery and openness to the Spirit of God.'[55] The World Cafe is built around a community meal, cooked by people who have often recently arrived in the city and want to engage with locals, learn about the culture and the people, but mostly want to feel free, simply to be themselves and share their own cultural riches. Thus, Rita says, 'we give a special welcome to all refugee and asylum seekers living in the city. Sharing a meal together is the focus of the World Cafe, where the food does not just feed our physical bodies, it also helps us to overcome our cultural, ethnic and religious prejudices.'

The cafe, like many projects, is not ecumenical by design but by happy accident and that seems to be reflective of the kind of grass roots unity where people are engaged in following the missionary Spirit together. Rita told me, 'The day Brexit vote happened in 2016 some felt worried, especially women, and some chose to stay indoors for a few days guessing or thinking that people will be nasty towards them. We do a lot of house visitations, the idea of the World Cafe is all about making relationships a priority where we see joy and sorrow.'[56]

When I asked her in an interview what she thought of the idea that she might be a gift her answer was, 'I have never thought of being a gift. I'm perhaps a prickly "gift"?'

Rita explained that the only Western people she experienced growing up behind the rusting iron curtain were the new missionaries who came in the wake of the collapse of communism in Lithuania after 1989. In her very early twenties she was part of a team that planted a new church. Her view of Western Christianity at that point was very rosy but changed when she arrived in the UK in the early noughties. Early on she noticed something she felt was unique:

> You have what I call a 'lovely' culture. It's all about 'loveliness'. Then I read the scripture and the culture of the New Testament much is not lovely. We Lithuanians are quite direct, and probably from an English perspective, blunt. It's

nice to be lovely but not all the time. As a Lithuanian I think
I bring a bit of a spicy taste which isn't usual for this culture.

Perhaps there is a 'loveliness' so ingrained in English culture
that we hardly notice it. That 'loveliness' might also be distin-
guished by its synonym 'niceness'. 'Niceness', at times, can be
a toxic English social strategy. It's a glaze. It's a surface-level
avoidance response. It's a painted-on smile, jolly along every-
body, nothing wrong here.

Growing up in Lithuania Rita explained she didn't have
faith:

As a country we are Roman Catholic. For Roman Catholics
suffering is like second breathing, you know? I'm guilty, I'm
guilty! You keep bashing yourself. Of course, my grandma
was Roman Catholic. I observed a lot of prayer during the
Soviet time and somehow with her friend she managed to
go to church all the time, and I think somehow she prayed
me into the presence of God. Later on in life as I became a
believer I see what she did for me.

My father was part of the Communist Party – many people
were. You had to be if you wanted to have any sort of a life
or a life for your kids. You had to join the Party and many
people did. Those who didn't struggled severely.

The best picture of faith I have is of my grandmother, my
mum's mum. She being devout and zealous, Catholic, going
to church every day – there was only one church left in our
city, the others turned into warehouses simply left to decay.
But there was something in culture – a hidden Christianity in
people's speech and their expressions.

Because I work with refugees I see a lot of injustice and
suffering and worries and bereavement and a sense of dislo-
cation. Of course, I'm joyful but I'm also a human being. As a
Lithuanian, the older I get the more I see grace and raw life in
people who perhaps don't have the faith that I claim to have
but there is something of God in them. When I observe their
lives I recognize that church is much bigger than the church I

am part of. Perhaps I can't call it church because they are not part of church but only God knows their hearts.

Rita, as a Lithuanian woman, is a gift to the Church in the UK. She has welcomed strangers into the World Cafe, welcomed them into the city of Gloucester. As someone who has lived through the collapse of communism and come and made her home among us, we have something to learn from her (and the many others who have chosen to walk a similar path).

'I'm a recovering missiologist' – Harvey

My friend Harvey Kwiyani calls himself a 'recovering missiologist' – it's easy to see why he might need some therapy. Koyama points out that if the aim of mission is the creation of a community centred by the peripheralized Christ, then the Church and Christian theology needs to be challenged, reoriented and honed by the voices and experiences of men and women from across the globe. What Koyama calls 'minority theologies' 'challenge the theological interpretations, formulations, symbolisations and liturgies of the dominant group that have been colonially and monoculturally presented and accepted'.[57]

Harvey is an important missiologist who previously taught at Liverpool Hope University in the Theology and Religious Studies Department for a number of years before being appointed (in September 2021) the CEO of Global Connections. For me, Harvey is someone who, if we listen to him, embodies this 'gift' and can enable us to see ourselves better.

As we spoke together one afternoon, Harvey said:

> I was born into the story of mission. By being born where I was born in Malawi you could not avoid the story. It is the story of my community and of my family. The land that was given to the missionaries in 1861 became Livingstone family colonial property in 1891. Those stories are deeply intertwined.

When we read mission history or study missiology up to doctoral level you discover there are stories (although you have to be intentional about it) by people who were colonized and evangelized by missionaries, and you have to ask a fundamental question – Is this really mission? I've been there. I have looked at the stories. I have read the accounts. Has this been hijacked and continues to be hijacked? It's in this sense that I think you know that the field as it is at the moment is not a field I want to identify with so I choose to step back. That was an easy decision for me to make because my experience in the UK has been that I teach African theology in a university because I couldn't land a role in a UK mission organization.

I created the journal *Missio Africanus*, I began to articulate some of thoughts on postcolonial missiology and the challenges, and then Liverpool Hope invited me to teach. But I couldn't find a space in any UK based mission organization to work from.

It's a lot of things. It's being a black African with a PhD in mission that many white people find threatening.

I asked Harvey why he thought white people found this threatening. He responded:

The simple answer is that as an African mission theologian and mission historian I know things that make some people uncomfortable. There is another side to the story of what we have taught in mission studies. There are historical facts that we need to face. We talk about mission as if these things never happened. For me, we can't move on until we have cleared it up and owned it. We might complain that theology is a white man's discipline, but missiology is even worse. There are so few alternative voices. It feels impossible – the field is still too colonial. So when I say I'm a recovering missiologist I'm critiquing the colonial history. I don't want to identify with that so I'm stepping back. I've been involved in mission studies for close to 20 years now. I've read and digested the literature but it's not a discipline I want to be identified with unless we own the history of colonialism which will lead us to a new missiology. That is difficult for many people to hear.

Harvey had this to say about the gift of the migrant in the UK context:

> This is not just about the UK or Europe, it's about humanity living together. No one community is self-contained. The starting point for me on this one is the Malawian proverb, 'a guest comes with a sharp penknife'. The background is an agrarian society with goats and cows. Occasionally a goat will get entangled in a bush and people will try to free it. They realize that someone among them, probably the stranger, will have a better penknife than them. It's a penknife because it's hidden. You have to ask for it. You extend hospitality to strangers because strangers will bring a fresh set of eyes.
>
> In the context of the UK, and for many migrants that have come to the UK, their coming has enriched the community. Migrants make a meaningful contribution to society. That is seen in all sorts of ways. But, more importantly, homogeneity is actually slow death. You have to mix the gene pool to keep the species going on a fundamentally biological level. But that can be expanded to ideas and theologies and expressions of Christianity.
>
> Yet it is very difficult for a black person to say you belong here totally in the UK. It doesn't matter if your parents came from Jamaica in 1948 or you've just arrived from Nigeria in 2018. You are an 'other' – immigrants will always say they are British, never that they are English.

Future church is intercultural church

With all that's been written above in mind, I want to suggest that the future Church will increasingly be expressed in intercultural ways. The flow of migration will continue in the UK context and communities will continue to be reshaped (however slowly) by the gift of migrant individuals and their related neighbourhoods. In the town where I live, I might choose to believe that it's 99 per cent made up of a white English community, but there are Polish, Romanian, Turkish, Indian and Chinese families slowly reshaping the landscape. A Kurdish man runs the local Italian delicatessen! Migration will continue to bring a dynamic challenge to many of our churches. In closing, I want to outline some important elements of what healthy intercultural life and ministry might look like.

For five years in Cape Town from 2013 to 2018 I had the joy and challenge of leading an inherited church congregation that could be considered intercultural, although it needed much attention – and intention – to push deeper into being genuinely so. Along with friends Idina and Mohan, I have written on what intercultural church looks like in specific contexts.[58] Here I share some theological and practical ideas of what it might look like to be intercultural.

First, good intercultural communities start with the understanding that the Great Commandment to love God and neighbour is at the heart of all safe, enriching and sustaining life. Paulas Budi Kleden says that good intercultural living is always rooted in loving Christ. Abiding and being rooted in the love of God is a precondition for successful interculturality. Kleden suggests that there are ten characteristics of God's love that act as the underpinning of intercultural life. I draw on a few here and share stories to concretize. Kleden says a characteristic of love is unconditional approval. In intercultural community we are called to accept that diversity of cultures is a blessing from God and meant for the richness for our society.[59] This in turn brings a freedom since genuine love is not a matter of calculation. Freedom is the important groundwork in which intercultural life needs to be placed. 'Intercultural is not a result of rational analysis but an act of freedom to accept, enrich and be enriched by others. It is an unconditional acceptance of other cultures.'[60]

However, intercultural life is not a passive acceptance of

people from other cultures.[61] Kleden points out that a characteristic of love is that it is active. We are therefore called to actively pursue friendship and relationship with others from different cultural backgrounds. Finding out about them, delighting in and making space for them at our tables, around the kitchen stove.

However, good intercultural community is often vulnerable and fragile. It is vulnerable and fragile because a characteristic of love is vulnerability. Living together is fraught with the possibility of miscommunicating and misunderstanding. Good intercultural community understands this and finds a route through without giving up because some were hurt in the past. 'Intercultural competence is gained when one is willing to go through these situations together.'[62] As Koyama knew, intercultural living is a call to conversion.

Finally, intercultural life must be guarded because there is always pressure from the dominant or majority culture towards homogeneity. Intercultural living or community doesn't aim at integration into the dominant or host culture. It rejoices at the gift each brings.

When I led St John's in Cape Town, we had a number of faithful members in the church who would lead intercessions. Some who had arrived at St John's, along the creases of the continent, were speakers of Kirundi, French, Kikongo, Swahili (the list is too long). Through the friendships in the church, they had learnt English and spoke it well. But I very much wanted my brothers and sisters to contribute to the life of our services, which were always in English, in their mother tongues as they led the body. The power and homogeneity of English as a default language had to be fought back time and time again. Jean Luc[63] would prepare his prayers starting in Kirundi but he might slip into English as he sensed people shuffling in their seats, sensing an unspoken pressure.

Making sure we sang together in languages other than English (there are 11 national languages in South Africa so there was really no excuse) was on occasions a battle. Sometimes singing in Swahili made us all learn new words since it is the unifying language of east Africa rather than South Africa. It made us all vulnerable as we attempted to pronounce new words and ways of being.

Many unaccompanied children from the local military base next to the church would join us every Sunday. Their first languages were almost always Xhosa, IsiZulu, Sotho, and at times English was their third language. Yet very often, white English-speaking adults could barely say their names. One morning a well-meaning woman asked a sweet young man beaming at her what his name was. After the fourth attempt to pronounce his name, she declared, 'I'm sorry that's impossible, I'll just call you John.' Intercultural living makes this unacceptable, and requires us to do deeper work with one another. Intercultural living means trying again until you get it right. Intercultural living is being prepared to make way, make room and space for others to thrive and live out of their culture without sensing it must be diluted or dialled down.

One day we decided to read the entire New Testament as a public act of worship in the many languages that were represented in our congregation. For 18 hours, from 6 a.m. one Saturday to midnight, we heard Scripture read aloud in French, German, Norwegian, Kirundi, IsiZulu, Xhosa, Danish, Shona and other languages. Some read slowly, almost painfully, others with gusto and full of theatrical skill. Some sat in the pews huddled in blankets, warmed by cups of tea and coffee. One Xhosa woman sat and listened for the entire day, refusing to move even for a bathroom break.

But the truest example of intercultural life, again imperfectly represented, was as we ate together. This was never more evident than on Heritage Day, celebrated on 24 September as a reminder that the nation of South Africa is made up of many peoples in a rich tapestry of cultures, typically, *braai-ing* (BBQ-ing) together. I still have a picture in my mind of a table full of men and women of different ages and races, some with stories of great pain and loss, eating and drinking together and laughing.

Conclusion

Extending hospitality to strangers is at the core of creating an authentic missiology. As I wrote the closing parts of this chapter, the news was filled with the stories of the Taliban taking city after city in Afghanistan, and when I came to editing it in readiness for publication Ukraine had been invaded by Russia. There are different responses to crises that affect human beings regardless of their religion and skin colour. There are likely to be other waves of migration as the climate continues to move into more catastrophic events that drive people from their homes and ways of life. Another wave of migrants is surely not too distant. The way society and the Church respond to migration and the gift of the other is a gauge of what we consider important. It reveals our love of God.

The future of the UK will be a more diverse landscape whatever the Home Secretary chooses to do. Welcoming, accepting, understanding, delighting in the gift of migrants is not a side issue; it is right at the centre of our missiology because it potentially has a global impact. Can we learn to live together with difference in a way that reflects something of the *shalom* of the coming kingdom? As Koyama says, the only way to stop the violence of genocide in our world is in the *via eminentiae* of extending hospitality to strangers as the Lamb of God did.[64]

Notes

1 John 4.34.

2 K. Koyama, 1997, 'My Pilgrimage in Mission', *International Bulletin of Missionary Research* 21(2), p. 58.

3 V. Erickson, 1996, 'Neighborology: A Feminist Ethno-Missiological Celebration of Kosuke Koyama' in D. Irvin and A. Akinade, *The Agitated Mind of God: The Theology of Kosuke Koyama*, Maryknoll, NY: Orbis Books, p. 154.

4 K. Koyama, 1979, *50 Meditations*, Maryknoll, NY: Orbis Books, p. 53.

5 K. Koyama, 1974, *Waterbuffalo Theology*, Maryknoll, NY: Orbis Books, p. 90.

6 Koyama, *50 Meditations*, p. 182.

7 K. Koyama, 1993, '"Extend Hospitality to Strangers" – A Missiology of Theologia Crucis', *International Review of Mission* 82(327), p. 288.

8 Koyama, '"Extend Hospitality to Strangers"', p. 286.

9 Koyama, '"Extend Hospitality to Strangers"', p. 284.

10 Koyama, '"Extend Hospitality to Strangers"', p. 284.

11 Koyama, '"Extend Hospitality to Strangers"', p. 284.

12 Koyama, '"Extend Hospitality to Strangers"', p. 286.

13 Koyama, '"Extend Hospitality to Strangers"', p. 285.

14 BBC, 2021, 'Canada: 751 unmarked graves found at residential school', *BBC News*, 24 June, https://www.bbc.co.uk/news/world-us-canada-57592243, accessed 31.3.2022.

15 E. Koss, 2021, 'A God who Wails and Dances: A Conversation with Yvonne Adhiambo Owuor', *Image Journal*, 109, https://imagejournal.org/article/a-god-who-wails-and-dances-a-conversation-with-yvonne-adhiambo-owuor/, accessed 31.3.2022.

16 K. Koyama, 1977, *No Handle on the Cross: An Asian Meditation on the Crucified Mind*, Eugene, OR: Wipf and Stock, p. 106.

17 Koyama, *No Handle on the Cross*, p. 34.

18 Koyama, *No Handle on the Cross*, p. 39.

19 D. Irvin, 2013, 'The Ritual of the Limping Dance: Kosuke Koyama's Positive Assessment of Pluralism for Christian Theology', *Journal of Ecumenical Studies* 48(3), p. 367.

20 G. Cuthbertson, 1988, 'The English-Speaking Churches and Colonialism' in C. Villa-Vicencio (ed.), *Theology and Violence: The South African Debate*, Grand Rapids, MI: Eerdmans, p. 22.

21 H. Kwiyani, 2020, 'Mission After George Floyd: On White Supremacy, Colonialism and World Christianity', *Anvil* 36(3), p. 7.

22 Kwiyani, 'Mission After George Floyd', p. 8.

23 Kwiyani, 'Mission After George Floyd', p. 9.

24 T. Maluleke, 2020, 'Racism *en Route*: An African Perspective', *The Ecumenical Review* 72, p. 27.

25 A. Jackelén, 2019, 'The Need for a Theology of Resilience, Co-existence and Hope', *The Ecumenical Review* 70(1–2), p. 14.

26 Jackelén, 'The Need for a Theology of Resilience, Coexistence and Hope', p. 15.

27 Jackelén, 'The Need for a Theology of Resilience, Coexistence and Hope', p. 15.

28 Home Office, 2022, 'Robin Simcox's Interim Term as Commissioner Extended', *Gov.uk*, 24 March, https://www.gov.uk/government/organisations/commission-for-countering-extremism, accessed 31.3.2022.

29 B. Lee, 2019, 'Overview of the Far-Right', Centre for Research and Evidence on Security Threats (CREST), p. 5 available at https://assets.publishing.service.gov.uk/government/uploads/system/uploads/attachment_data/file/816692/Ben_Lee_-_Overview_of_the_far_right.pdf, accessed 23.7.2019.

30 J. Welby, 2018, *Reimagining Britain: Foundations for Hope*, London: Bloomsbury Continuum, p. 2.

31 O. Bell, 2018, 'The British Exceptionalism Delusion', *Epicurus Today*, 5 March, https://epicurus.today/the-british-exceptionalism-delusion/, accessed 31.3.2022.

32 J. Harris, 2020, 'We can't hide behind the bunting – let's face up to what's happened to Britain', *The Guardian*, 11 May, https://www.theguardian.com/commentisfree/2020/may/11/bunting-britain-covid-19-crisis-nationalist, accessed 31.3.2022.

33 K. Koyama, 2003, 'Reformation in the Global Context: The Disturbing Spaciousness of Jesus Christ', *Currents in Theology and Mission* 30(2), p. 123.

34 BBC, 2020, 'Katherine Johnson: Hidden Figures Nasa mathematician dies at 101', *BBC News*, 24 February, https://www.bbc.co.uk/news/world-us-canada-51619848, accessed 31.3.2022.

35 C. Collins, 2020, 'In What Ways Can the Present-day Methodist Church in Britain be Described as "Prophetic" in the Sense that John Hull Uses the Term?', unpublished MA thesis.

36 D. Dorling and S. Tomlinson, 2019, *Rule Britannia: Brexit and the End of Empire*, London: Biteback Publishing, p. 41.

37 Dorling and Tomlinson, *Rule Britannia*, p. 42.

38 A. Reddie, 2018, 'Now You See me, Now You Don't: Subjectivity, Blackness, and Difference in Practical Theology in Britain post Brexit', *Practical Theology* 11(1), pp. 4–16.

39 L. Bretherton, 2016, 'Brexit as Theodicy and Idolatry', *ABC*, 25 June, https://www.abc.net.au/religion/brexit-as-theodicy-and-idolatry/10096834, accessed 31.2.2022.

40 J. Stone, 2016, 'Nigel Farage backtracks on Leave campaign's "£350m for the NHS" pledge hours after result', *The Independent*, 25 June, https://www.independent.co.uk/news/uk/politics/eu-referendum-result-nigel-farage-nhs-pledge-disowns-350-million-pounds-a7099906.html, accessed 31.3.2022.

41 J. Stone, 2018, 'British public still believe Vote Leave "£350million a week to EU" myth from Brexit referendum', *The Independent*, 28 October, https://www.independent.co.uk/news/uk/politics/vote-leave-brexit-lies-eu-pay-money-remain-poll-boris-johnson-a8603646.html, accessed 31.3.2022.

42 Jackelén, 'The Need for a Theology of Resilience, Coexistence and Hope', p. 15.

43 B. Quinn, 2019, 'Hate crimes double in five years in England and Wales', *The Guardian*, 15 October, https://www.theguardian.com/society/2019/oct/15/hate-crimes-double-england-wales, accessed 31.3.2022.

44 Home Office, 2019, 'Hate Crime, England and Wales, 2018/19', Home Office, https://assets.publishing.service.gov.uk/government/uploads/system/uploads/attachment_data/file/839172/hate-crime-1819-hosb2419.pdf, accessed 31.3.2022.

45 F. A. Walls, 2014, 'Mission and Migration: The Diaspora Factor in Christian History' in C. H. Im and A. Yong (eds), *Global Diasporas and Mission*, Oxford: Regnum, p. 19.

46 K. Koyama, 1982, 'Christ at the Periphery', *The Ecumenical Review* 34(1), p. 71.

47 Dorling and Tomlinson, *Rule Britannia*, p. 38.

48 D. Olusoga, *Black and British: A Forgotten History*, London: Pan Macmillan.

49 Walls, 'Mission and Migration', p. 33.

50 Walls, 'Mission and Migration', p. 34.

51 H. Sherwood, 2020, 'Church of England urged to apologise for Windrush racism', *BBC News*, 24 January, https://www.theguardian.com/world/2020/jan/24/church-of-england-urged-to-apologise-for-windrush-racism, accessed 31.3.2022.

52 Walls, 'Mission and Migration', p. 35.

53 A. Herman and C. Burlacioiu, 2016, 'Current Debates About the Approach of the "Munich School" and Further Perspectives on the Interdisciplinary Study of the History of World Christianity', *Journal of World Christianity* 6(1), p. 70.

54 ECM, 'Vidas & Rita Rimkus', *European Christian Mission*, https://www.ecmi.org/en/worker-detailpage/6915f209-16d3-4784-952f-3288cf98559a, accessed 31.3.2022.

55 ECM, 'Vidas & Rita Rimkus'.

56 Personal email to author dated 7 February 2020.

57 Koyama, '"Extend Hospitality to Strangers"', p. 288.

58 B. Aldous, I. Dunmore and M. Seevaratnam, 2021, *Intercultural Church: Shared Learning from New Communities*, Cambridge: Grove Books.

59 P. Kleden, 2020, 'The Love of Christ Impels Us' in L. Stanislaus and C. Tauchner (eds), *Becoming Intercultural: Perspectives on Mission*, New Delhi: iSPCK, p. 11.

60 Kleden, 'The Love of Christ Impels Us', p. 11.

61 Kleden, 'The Love of Christ Impels Us', p. 12.

62 Kleden, 'The Love of Christ Impels Us', p. 14.

63 The name is anonymized here.

64 Kleden, 'The Love of Christ Impels Us', p. 286.

4

Talking:
Shut Up and Listen, Will You!

Introduction

In his lifetime Jesus walked slowly from village to village, stopping to teach and engage with people as the landscape provided opportunity. He listened to a woman at the well and shifted her thinking about the Messiah. He discerned people's hearts and taught in such a way that his listeners were confronted with their hardened attitudes. Jesus, so alive to the Holy Spirit, was able to discern at every point and in every person the deepest, profoundest need. Yet Jesus treated each person with dignity and respect while graciously challenging, gently provoking and lovingly drawing them to see both themselves and himself in deeper ways. In all these interactions Jesus helped to pull theology out of people's lives, and in doing so enabled them to discover who he was and who they could become.

When I arrived in post at the church in Cape Town I took over the generic email address of the previous minister. With it I inherited all the email subscriptions he had signed up to over the years. Many I unsubscribed from within the first month or so but one I found fascinating and decided to keep receiving it. Let's say it was from 'Victory Crusade for Africa Ministries'. That's not too far from being accurate but is as non-specific as is possible. Towards the end of each month I would receive an email updating me on the number of souls won over in the previous four weeks or so. The number was often included in the email title and was never less than 1,000. It was always specific

95

in terms of numbers – a set of statistics telling me which sub-
Saharan nation has the most 'wins' – something akin to the
sales tallies for the number of shoes sold by Clarks in the
counties of the south west of England. Who was doing better?
Who was riding high in the salvation charts? I often wondered
who these men, women and children really were. Rarely did I
glimpse from these emails who the dear precious people behind
the numbers really were. But it was clear that this was essentially a numbers game.

In this chapter I want to explore evangelism in the UK context and ask what we might learn from a number of Koyama's
ideas. As with many of Koyama's writings, we never encounter a fully a laid out and developed theology of evangelism.
Dale Irvin insists that Koyama 'often found himself asking in
various ways the question: What is the mission of the Christian
church today?'[1] However, Koyama rarely did this in systematic and obvious ways. Instead, he would fashion a meditation
on a particular topic and ask what the implications for our
evangelism might be, almost as an aside.

While this may be the case with Koyama, it doesn't mean
that there are not fundamental starting points that we may
use to construct theologies of evangelism. I think there are
three (although there are doubtless many more) key themes in
Koyama's writings that we may use to reflect on evangelism in
the UK context today.

The first starting point is the statement that 'Christianity
suffers from teacher complex'. Koyama begins his most suc-
cinct reflection on evangelism by stating that the future of
Christianity was in jeopardy. He says that, 'Christianity has
become so self-righteous that I do not see much future for it.
It wants to teach. It does not want to learn. It is arrogant. It
is suffering from teacher complex.'[2] Koyama reminds us that
Christianity and Jesus Christ are not the same thing and that
there is 'no such thing as a divine, pure and uncontaminated
Christianity'. Koyama argues that for 400 years Christianity
has not really listened to the peoples of Asia – and I guess,
by extension, Africa, South America, and the multiplicity of

indigenous cultures across the globe. Christianity has been too 'busy planning mission strategy'. People have become the objects of evangelism.[3] Yet, Koyama says, Jesus was good at listening and asking questions. 'In the gospels, don't we get the strong impression that Jesus was not a talkative man, but he was a careful listener?'[4] So to begin we may need an evangelism where we relinquish the posture of the teacher. Perhaps we need to explore an evangelism of listening?

A second starting point is that the Church needs to become a church that enters the world with mutilated hands rather than attractive hands. Koyama implores the Church to be present as 'inefficient' and 'crucified' like its Lord, rather than stream-lined and polished. The Church does not need to create happy customers but pilgrims on the way. Koyama says that, 'Jesus as the crucified one comes not with grasping hands but with open hands revealing his wounds.' To me it is fascinating that his resurrection body still bore the marks of his crucifixion. We might ask the question, 'Why does the Church not reflect this woundedness more, in its prime witness to the world?' Perhaps we need an evangelism of the stigma of Jesus?

A third starting point that is interrelated to, and draws richly from, the previous point is that Koyama advocated an evangelism that was rooted in *theologia crucis* and Christ at the periphery. Meditations on the 'inefficiency' of the crucified one weave their way through every book Koyama wrote and almost every article and speech he gave. Koyama sought to shed light on the problem of the 'crusading' mind and the need for it to be replaced by the 'crucified' mind. Too much of Christian mission history is inextricably linked to a crusading mindset, as we saw partially in the last chapter. Meditation on *theologis crucis* is right at the heart of the questions that Koyama posed for the Church in regard to mission and evangelism. David Thang Moe suggests that Koyama's theology is 'Christocentric through and through. Building on a theology of the cross, he took Christology to be the centre for his missiology.'[5] Koyama continually argued that while Christ occupies the centre he always moves towards the periphery. 'Jesus Christ is the centre becoming periphery. He affirms his centrality. That is what this designation "crucified Lord" means. His life moves towards the periphery. Finally, on the cross he stops this movement.'[6]

Koyama says that to make contact with the centre is to come into contact with salvation.[7] However, while Christ can rightfully occupy this position he chooses to journey towards the edge, the margins, the periphery. In fact, Christ affirms his centrality by giving it up for the sake of the periphery.[8] Koyama goes so far as to suggest that all 'our thoughts on mission and evangelism must be examined in the light of the periphery-orientated authority of Jesus Christ'.[9]

In this move to the periphery, Koyama says that it is the broken Christ who heals the world broken by idolatry.[10] He found it difficult to reconcile the idea of a prestigious and powerful church proclaiming the crucified Christ. For Koyama, Jesus Christ is at the centre of the biblical message for Christians, yet he could say 'the theological meaning of the brokenness in the depth of work and person of Jesus Christ has been ignored'.[11] Admitting that this concept of a broken Christ is not a source for meditation because we don't like weakness and pain, Koyama suggests that new space is created at the cost of the life of Christ. Perhaps we need an evangelism of the periphery or 'spat-upon' evangelism?

Using these starting points we may want to ask the following questions. What if evangelism is more about listening than talking? What if evangelism is less about delivering theological factoids and more about asking pertinent questions born out of love and discernment? What if our success is to be measured less by numbers and statistics, charting progress along the Engel's scale,[12] and more about pilgrimage and soul friendship based on mutual learning and deep reciprocity? What if we were truly prepared to embrace slowness as we build relationships with people? How does our evangelism reveal the inefficiency, humiliation, brokenness of the crucified Christ? Put more simply, we must learn, as Stefan Paas challenges us, 'to be weak, foolish and hopeful in the world'.[13]

Quo vadis evangelism?

Why does it occasionally feel that an evangelistic encounter is something akin to a visit by a sales rep from a double-glazing company? A few years ago, I had a visit from a sales executive to replace a secondary front door in the old bookshop where I live. I showed him what needed to be replaced and anticipated a number of questions about exactly what I required. As I might have expected, I was met with a sales spiel. Ted had clearly memorized a text to be regurgitated in a particular sequence. It included asking me if I knew certain technical information about wood, paint bonding, and other industrialized processes that go into preparing a new door (which I obviously didn't) and allowed him to move on to his next glazing factoid taking no notice of whether this was helpful or even relevant to me. We got to the point where he asked me what type of letter box and door handle and locking system I wanted. I explained it was a false door so it didn't need any of those things. He was stunned, bewildered that he hadn't realized, and walked around the room scratching his head trying to work out what came next. During his pitch he had completely missed what I was actually asking for because he was so concerned about delivering to me the 'important' information.

It can feel like this in the worst kind of evangelistic encounter. An evangelistic sales rep who is delivering using the correct terms with a couple of theological words thrown in. As I sometimes walk from our CTE offices in London there is often a man on the corner of Oxford Street and Charing Cross Road with a loudspeaker strapped to his chest telling all passers-by that Jesus had died for them and by shedding his blood on the cross had made peace with God. 'Have faith in Jesus,' he urged the confused onlookers over and again. While on one level I have no objection with the contents of the message I have major problems with the medium. The medium is the message. It's what my friend Sanjee Perera calls 'monological missiology'. It's the kind of one-way traffic that consistently turns people off. Koyama knew this and said that 'the teacher-complex tends to be powered by a one way traffic psychology'.[14]

Alternatively, I hope to show that the kind of evangelism I think Koyama was advocating is rooted in listening, acknowledging, loving, being and suffering with, lamenting alongside, and most often – though not always – it will be slow.

However, we must admit that there is often a lack of confidence and at times profound uncertainty around evangelism for many in the churches. One senior leader I was on a call with during the coronavirus lockdown said to me he wondered what the Church had been doing for the last 50 years when so many who faithfully attend church each week were still totally ill equipped to share their faith with others. As revealed by an email I received from someone in Churches Together circles in early 2021, having received an email from me about an evangelism initiative, Karen[15] wrote hesitantly:

> The reason for this email is a bit difficult to articulate but essentially what I am interested in is WHY do we want to introduce people to Jesus/re-engage folk who have drifted away etc. I get sent lots of materials but no one ever explains about the 'why'. The bottom line is – what difference does it make? WHY do we want people to know about Jesus? Another way of asking the same question might be – in what way(s) is a Christian's life more meaningful and invigorated than that of a non-Christian? I find that increasingly difficult to answer.

In this honest response Karen is not alone in her wrestle as to *why* we want to engage people. She articulates a problem that many sit with. As we exchanged emails it became clear that she had problems with any exclusive claims about Jesus. Jesus was another option in the pantheon, and exclusive claims about him were insulting to those of other faiths or none. Karen articulated for me a dilemma that many have. It's a dilemma Stephan Paas comments on, suggesting that being called into the mission of God in post-Christian Europe can feel at the very least an unsuccessful project or like joining a lost cause.[16] It seems to be how Karen felt.

But that dilemma also partly arises from misconceptions and suspicions around evangelism. In our pluralistic, multicultural and multifaith society we may ask if our evangelism is morally dubious or indeed irrelevant as Karen did. A casual scroll through Amazon's results on evangelism gives us a plethora of adjectival suffixes. Evangelism might be *Questioning, Honest, Natural, Power-oriented, Mystic, Celtic, Biblical, Postmodern* and *Mission-shaped* and so forth. All these approaches are valid and valuable. There are certainly many resources for all sorts of people in all sorts of settings. And yet often it's still a word whispered in low tones by church leaders and lay people alike. A leader of a major church-planting organization emailed me recently to say they were doing a new series on the 'E' word. We both knew what he meant. At least I think we did.

So, what has happened and what should be happening? My friend Harvey Kwiyani, the Malawian missiologist, mused upon the future, stating, 'the type of evangelisation that will speak to Westerners will have to be apologetic in its approach, humble in its outlook, and less confident in its posture and its truth claims'.[17] I think that echoes much of what Koyama stood for and implored the Church to grasp.

Evangelism, evangelization and witness

Terms are important mostly because it tends to be that everyone thinks everyone else knows what they mean when they use a particular word. Evangelism, evangelization and witness are words that can often, and invariably do, get used interchangeably. Andrew Kirk suggests that the words 'evangelism' and 'evangelization' should be used interchangeably as 'attempts to distinguish their respective meanings have not proved particularly useful'.[18] In the Greek the *evangel* was about the announcement or publishing of good news. Usually that word is translated in the New Testament as 'gospel'. In English Bible translations, *evangelion* is usually translated as 'gospel' and *evangelizesthai/evangelisein* as 'preach the gospel'.

From a Roman Catholic perspective, 'the Second Vatican Council (1962–1965) ushered in a paradigm shift in the theology of mission. Its emphasis moved from "missions" to "mission" and then toward "evangelization".'[19] Some Catholics retain the use of the word 'evangelization', while others – like the Sion Community[20] – have decided to use the term 'evangelism' to describe their activities. Evangelization tends to have a much broader whole-life orientation rather than being situated in the sometimes narrow confines of evangelism, which can be overly focused on proclamation. In *Evangelii nuntiandi* Pope John Paul II writes that:

> evangelization involves an explicit message, adapted to the different situations constantly being realized, about the rights and duties of every human being, about family life without which personal growth and development is hardly possible, about life in society, about international life, peace, justice and development – a message especially energetic today about liberation.[21]

The width and life-wide emphasis of evangelization is perhaps closer to the Hebrew concept of *shalom*. Evangelization then sees the impact of the Christ story on every sphere of life – spiritual, social, cultural and political. Generally, the Orthodox family of churches have tended to use the term 'witness' rather than 'evangelism' as those like Ion Bria and others see common witness as an extension and outflow of the liturgy. 'Orthodox people have not only integrated eucharist liturgy into their piety, but also they have made the eucharist a vital element of their witness and mission.'[22] Although Bosch[23] argues that Protestants prefer the word 'evangelization' in contemporary Britain the term 'evangelism' is most often used by Evangelicals, Pentecostals and Charismatics.

Witness, the preferred language for the Orthodox, conjures up a more humbled image given the relationship between the

Greek word *martureo* and 'martyr' in the English. To witness is to expect or embrace death, metaphorically at the very least. For many across the world it is an ongoing reality. For those ancient Orthodox communities in Egypt, Iran, Iraq and Syria, witness and martyrdom have a recent and devastating impact. The kidnapping and beheading of 21 Coptic Christians by IS in Libya in 2015 is one such example.[24] Other examples can be found among the members of the Holy Catholic Apostolic Assyrian Church of the East in Iraq and the Malankara Mar Thoma Syrian Church in India. In all these contexts the Church finds itself at the margins of society despised, ignored, ostracized and brutalized. They experience 'a spat-upon evangelism' that few of us in the relative comfort and luxury of the global north can imagine. Might we have something to learn from them?

Evangelism and the empire

Peter Cruchley-Jones notes that often the contemporary Church has not detected the inherent irony in the early Church in adopting the language and concept of *evangelion*. This is an irony we have not inhabited. It was the PR of empire, the announcement of good news of victory. As the imperial cult took hold, it was the standard word for any announcement of auspicious news about the emperor and the imperial family. Using this term was meant to be a satire of empire and the beginnings of the counter-imperial movement that was the early Church. The *evangelion*, the gospel, begins not as information, but as action, efficacious power that enters into the world to save and transform.[25] Many of us have not detected this irony or inhabited it as churches. We continue to operate too often as willing partners with empire, which situates us at the centre – giving us power and authority to proclaim.

From evangelism as proclamation to contextual theologies

Beth Keith gives a helpful overview of the prevailing shifts in attitudes towards evangelism suggesting that evangelism as proclamation has been subdued as a result of the rise of pluralism and secularization, and replaced by contextual approaches. 'The perceived failure of the "Decade of Evangelism" in the 1990s followed by the rise in contextualisation, and an increasingly post-Christian context which encourages civility and tolerance, have together contributed to the shift away from evangelism as proclamation.'[26] The decade probably had a limited impact on the Church in terms of halting decline and it was viewed by some parts of the global Communion as having achieved little. Former Archbishop of Canterbury Rowan Williams called the decade 'a necessary idiocy' and stated that 'much of Western Christianity has gone to sleep on the job'. For Williams, evangelism is so much the essence of the Church that a decade of evangelism was rather like declaring a decade of breathing.[27]

While the pertinence of these shifts is debatable, Keith's exploration of the shift in evangelism from proclamation to contextual is important. Both Keith and Paas suggest that the Christian West continues to experience increasing marginalization. 'Evangelism stands in the shadow of the shameful history of colonialism, TV preachers and religious wars,'[28] says Keith. This shift from proclamation to contextual is revealed for Keith by a lack of serious literature on proclamation over the past 20 years and a dearth of serious theological reflection on evangelism.[29]

Contextual forms of mission advocated by the fresh expressions and other movements associated with it tend to take a much softer approach to evangelism. As it is committed to listening, loving and service as the primary ways of engaging a community, discipleship and forming worshipping communities can come a lot later on in the journey or, to the dismay of many, not at all. The problem of the great omission of evangelism as a central part of contextual approaches is so apparent that in September 2021 Fresh Expressions in the UK launched a new resource called Sharing Jesus.[30] This corrective is important for missional movements, some of which Paas says 'do not seem to be rooted in a clear and convincing theology of salvation'.[31] He says that while some missional communities desire to initiate newcomers into Christianity they often don't see how this can happen. I don't propose to offer any simple solution to this thorny problem other than to highlight its existence. In the remainder of this chapter, I want to explore three approaches to evangelism rooted in Koyama and share stories of how these look in real life.

Evangelism as listening

If, as Koyama suggests, the Church has neglected to listen and has a teacher complex then what might an evangelism of listening look like? First, do we really have a problem? In a world shaped by a hyper abundance of words and images, perhaps we have been numbed. How much of our experience in daily life is a bombardment of words written and spoken? It can feel at times as if we float in a never-ending sea of verbiage. Along with a desire to tap into slowness as outlined in Chapter 2, and acknowledgement that speed is killing us, there is a growing need from many of us for silence, a posture of stillness and less talk.

Italian philosopher Gemma Corradi Fiumara traces the way in which Western forms of knowledge have by and large not fostered a posture of listening. Fuimara says that 'the more rigorous knowledge claims are, the more "greedily" they demand to be listened to'.[32] But more than that, 'when western knowledge tries to frame the entire world and its history by making use of power that emanates from the voice of our rationality, then, perhaps, our excessively logocentric culture emerges in which there is no longer any room for listening'.[33] Susan Hedahl notes that Fuimara is in fact claiming that the

adaptation of a philosophy of listening will rattle, if not re-
arrange, our epistemological cage to the extent that we are
led to another form of rationality.[34] Western Christianity is so
closely tied to, and inhabited by, Greek forms of rationality
that it might be said to have squeezed out listening. While there
has been much theological reflection on Christological kenosis
rooted in the hymn from Philippians 2, we may also need to
reflect on a kenosis of words.

Recovering listening

If we insist that evangelism is listening, we automatically
run into trouble. If evangelism is essentially understood as
proclamation and fundamentally rooted in words and speech,
we are confronted with a seemingly insurmountable problem
right from the start. How can evangelism really be listening?
We may start with listening but many of us are programmed to
formulate our answer as soon as the speaker commences. Subconsciously we are assessing an acceptable time period before
we may set off and begin again.

The very idea of evangelism as listening will be difficult for
many. In my work at CTE I host and facilitate a forum called the
Group for Evangelisation.[35] It brings together national denominational leaders with the portfolio for evangelism, including
charities and theological education institutions, a forum to
share news, reflect and consider ways to collaborate together.
A number of folk who attend are out and out evangelists.
They are the type of people who have been doing public street
preaching for 40 years, are involved in evangelistic stand-up
comedy at the Edinburgh Festival Fringe, or are continually
producing brilliant resources to help ordinary Christians share
their faith. I'm sure many of them would be bewildered – or
at the very least grimacing – reading these words. They might
concede it starts with listening but pretty quickly it's about
talking and proclaiming. How else will people hear unless we
speak?

But in a world with a hyper abundance of words, might our over-exposure lead to a devaluing of language and meaning? Words can have decayed meaning and fall into cliché. I want to suggest that a recovery of listening will be dependent on us being less concerned about time and more concerned with people, posture and presence. Pope Francis in *Evangelii gaudium* reminds us that 'evangelization consists mostly of patience and disregard for constraints of time'.[36] Or as the Apostle James reminds us, we should 'be quick to listen and slow to speak'.[37] It's difficult to over-emphasize quite how difficult this is for many of us convinced at the truth of the gospel to not talk but to listen.

Sara Savage has helpfully linked listening to love, suggesting that 'the experience of being listened to is so close to the experience of being loved as to be indistinguishable'.[38] If listening and love are so closely intertwined, then deep listening and presence can be seen as acts of love utterly foundational before any kind of words or speech may be necessary. We need to acknowledge the power of asking the right questions and living the answers.

Elaine Heath says that a hermeneutic of love is grounded in the belief that Jesus really does live in the people around us and really does thirst for them. In a hermeneutic of love Heath says, 'I give myself in prayer and friendship to the people around me, not so I can get something from them, not even a commitment to join my church but so that I can minister to Jesus in them.'[39] An evangelism shaped by listening and a commitment to a hermeneutic of love is rooted in the *imago Dei*, a resolute determination not to objectify or commodify anybody but rather to be attentive to the image of God within each person.

There is evidence that listening is coming to the fore in many movements. The concept of 'missional listening' is a fundamental initial component of *pioneer* ministry. Examples of missional listening abound but often I have been struck by the time that listening can take. Listening is not to be a rushed exercise. That is why pioneer mission models and postures ungird all surface activity to be rooted in continual twin disciplines of prayer and listening. I've heard stories where listening before deciding on any concrete action in a particular location took over a decade.

Missional listening is a 360-degree activity – the term has been developed out of the idea of double listening originally conceived by John Stott and a feature of the 2004 *Mission-shaped Church* report. Fresh Expressions have developed this posture into a 360-degree activity, as Mike Moynagh explains: 'This is listening in a round – getting your bearings from all fours points of the compass.'[40] The Partnership for Missional Church (PMC) is an excellent example rooted in deep and profound listening. It is a three-year process of deep culture change that helps churches reconnect with their communities and, with the call of God through embedding new spiritual practices, taking the time to listen to their communities, and developing collaborative mission projects to meet the needs of local people. The first year of this process enables church members, through a set of habitual spiritual practices and some specific listening and discovery tasks, to listen deeply to God, to one another and their local community. While these notions of missional listening bring together context, history, prayer and Scripture in the listening process for community I don't see why we may not carry this over into the realm of the individual person which takes absolutely seriously the *imago Dei*.

Listening needs recovery in our evangelism and mission more than ever if we are to undo the centuries (400 of them and more) of the empire violence of not listening. In true listening we allow the other to set the agenda, and ask the questions that are at the root of their experience in searching for God. But almost perversely, in listening we must also be prepared to be told we are not needed, wanted or appreciated. In essence, we cannot only listen to the things we want to hear or we agree with.

Apophatic evangelism

In Christian theology there is a long tradition among the mystics and early Church Fathers of recognizing our limitations in knowing. Listening may also be a pathway to the apophatic. By eschewing words and focusing on listening we are acknowledging the inadequacy of all language in encountering the one beyond all words. The one beyond all names and all naming. As Peter Rollins has noted, we need to be better at understanding 'how not to speak of God'.[41] Apophatic theology does not insist that we know nothing about God but recognizes our epistemological frailty. We see through a glass darkly. Our God talk is limited, partial and fragmented. God cannot be examined as another object under the microscope – which is the failure of enlightenment rationalism – for while God is within the world God is beyond all.

For the mystics, God was encountered in the cloud of unknowing. Writers such as St John of the Cross and Meister Eckhart used language like nothingness, darkness, emptiness and detachment to describe their encounters with the one beyond all words. For many, these terms are connected to silence. Silence is the beginning of listening. Silence of course is a difficult concept to situate in the midst of proclamation and yet of course it was the line of action Jesus takes at a time when he probably was most tempted by some kind of self-assertion or self-justification. In the passion narratives Christ chooses time and again not to give a full account of himself to accusers – the bewildered and incredulous Pilate, among others. 'Like a sheep before its shearers is silent, so he opened not his mouth.' Again, silence has different types of qualities. Silence can be oppressive and coercive, forcing someone to keep their mouth shut or not to speak out. That can be a malignant and destructive silence. But silence can also open up a space to the one beyond all words – in this we need to 'read' the quality of silence. Is not the mystery of Christ and the incomprehensible nature of the work of Jesus beyond mere words, however eloquent and well crafted? Is there a role for silence in pointing to the mystery of Christ? As Koyama points out in his 1980 address at the WCC conference in Melbourne, 'All the world becomes silent and all human powers are challenged by the profound sincerity of the crucified Christ.'[42]

Perhaps Bonhoeffer's idea of religionless Christianity and the need for the Church to be silent until it has a new language in a 'world come of age' can help us here? In his *Letters and Papers from Prison*[43] Bonhoeffer gropes towards a religionless Christianity, which from his perspective leads to a necessary silence. He asks, 'What do a church, a community, a sermon, a liturgy, a Christian life mean in a religionless world? How do we speak of God – without religion, i.e. without the temporally conditioned presuppositions of metaphysics, inwardness, and so on? How do we speak (or perhaps we cannot now even "speak" as we used to).'[44] In our post-Christendom context perhaps we need to be much more thoughtful about the idea of not being able to speak as we used to?

Rowan Williams helps me to explore the inherent tension and seeming dichotomy of silence and speech. He points out that the world is a place where it is barely possible to speak without making things more difficult and destructive. Rather, he says the commonwealth of God is a place where speech is restored in praise, patience and attentive speaking. But coupled with that is a silence as an *expectant quiet*, the quiet before the dawn when we don't want to say anything too quickly for fear of spoiling what is uncovered as the light comes.[45] Might we be able to develop an apophatic evangelism, rooted in silence and listening? In some parts of the Church this will be difficult to comprehend and probably be rejected outright. We have a gospel to proclaim, but who can proclaim – and how – also needs some examination. In our logocentric, so full of words, world how might we learn from those at the margins, vulnerable and sometimes seemingly dislocated from their participation in the mission of God.

In a compelling article the Indonesian feminist and disability theologian Isabella Novsima explores something of apophatic mission based on research among some of the most marginalized in the global south. Novsima sets out a place for non-verbal mission using the example of women with intellectual disabilities in the Indonesian context. She asks us to imagine the kind of witness someone is if they are unable to speak in the same way as an able-bodied person. She says:

> Can a person with intellectual disabilities be a witness in the Christian mission? If we understand mission only cataphatically, it clearly becomes impossible to consider a person with intellectual disabilities as a witness, since the standard is laden with logocentrism, where language and knowledge are centred on words.[46]

Yet Novsima argues in the divine grace of the *missio Dei* no one is excluded on these grounds. She suggests that self-expressing as a form of witness is beyond words. 'There might be ways that people with intellectual disabilities can express themselves using what they already have, and those ways could be non-verbal.'[47] That may be in ways we might not usually associate with evangelism. Being a witness in this way I think is closely related to Koyama's idea of mission being doxology. It's something that Stefan Paas suggests too. If we are marginalized, vulnerable or easily dismissed in the world, then our praise will look strange, useless, insignificant and possibly bewildering. Maybe, but it is the core of our identity in evangelism. Paas says that 'doxological mission helps Christians deal with their weakness and fatigue'.[48] Moreover, when Christians praise God they say something like this: 'There is One who is not good for anything, but who is simply good. Period.' Why must words be at the centre of that communication?

I have a nephew named Ollie. He is nine years old. He was born with Down's syndrome. Over the years Ollie has learnt to communicate well but his words are sometimes difficult to understand, even for his loving parents who know him most intimately. I remember arriving at the hospital a few hours after Ollie was born. His parents had chosen not to have the screening that detects trisomy 21 around 10–14 weeks into a pregnancy. When Ollie was delivered, they were surprised (in a good way). Ollie is a gift to the immediate and extended family. A gift that has pushed them into spaces and situations that have at times been challenging and at times dismaying. As he has grown, he has shown a particular passion for worship music. I'm probably better known as 'Ben guitar' than Uncle Ben. The local church family in Durban, South Africa, have embraced this wholeheartedly. Every week Ollie takes his personally marked microphone and stands at the front with the worship bands and helps lead. He is not dismissed or told to move out of the way. He is embraced and invited to take his place as part of God's people. His uninhibited praise is a witness to the church community and to the wider world. But more than his praise, Ollie has a profound discernment for sensing pain (mental anguish, dismay and grief for example) in people during church services. My sister-in-law Sarah wrote, 'Ollie always finds people in pain during the worship service and will stay with them and minister just by his physical presence.' She continued, 'I have so many stories of people in our church of how this has blessed and ministered to them. In it he offers what he can out of what others may perceive as a profound lack or vulnerability. Profound vulnerability is right at the heart of the gospel narrative.'

In a similar vein, John Swinton offers a wonderful story which narrates the power of vulnerability and wordlessness.[49] As part of a research project on spirituality and profound intellectual disability, John and his colleague Susannah got to know a 13-year-old girl, Katie. Katie was born with Sturge-Weber syndrome. In Sturge-Weber syndrome, facial birthmarks extend over the brain and can cause restrictions in movement and also seizures. Katie's communication was very limited; she only had a few words yet was actively involved in her school and enjoyed attending Girls' Brigade. One evening at the club one of the leaders fell over and hurt her foot so badly she was unable to walk. The children were asked if they would like to pray for healing. Katie immediately raised her hand. The group closed their eyes and Katie led a wordless prayer. When the leader returned to the doctor for a check-up she was told that the foot had healed unusually well despite the initial severity. Katie's prayer, silent as it appeared, had a profound consequence.

Novsima reminds us that 'vulnerability is the heart of the Christian mission. It disrupts logocentrism, which maintains the empire of language and knowledge, the words and the cognition.'[50] As Paul reminds us in 2 Corinthians, 'that is why, for Christ's sake, I delight in weaknesses, in insults, in hardships, in persecutions, in difficulties. For when I am weak, then I am strong.' I don't think we have even begun to seriously reflect on the centrality of vulnerability in our evangelistic endeavours. Yet it's in our vulnerability and weakness that we are shaped for empathy, mercy and compassion for others. When that becomes axiomatic in our approaches to evangelism, it will be impossible just to see people as our projects. Our love for them regardless of their response will be overflowing. Far too often the narratives portrayed are the strong, now redeemed, well adjusted, conquerers of sin and death imparting the good news. Can we learn to inhabit our vulnerabilities rather than see them as something to be pushed aside? Can we stop ourselves offering words when silence may be the best discerned alternative?

Stigma of Jesus evangelism

I think this leads into this idea of the stigma of Jesus evangelism. Koyama believed that the 'whole gospel radiated from the self-denial of Jesus Christ'.[51] Koyama felt that too often the Church didn't fully understand the call to live with the *stigma* of Jesus Christ. 'Do we live with this sign? Is our life continuously made uneasy and insecure (!) because of the *stigma* we bear?' Koyama asks. He compares this question against the Buddhist monk whom he had befriended in Singapore: 'His orange robes and empty bag point to the ideal of monastic life, the value of homelessness that Buddha taught.'[52] By comparison, Koyama felt that too often the 'church lived comfortably on the side of the governing authorities who do not understand the glory of the crucified Christ'.[53] He compares what he calls the security-minded and budget-minded Protestant missionaries to his friend the monk and asks if it is possible that the monk is closer to the *stigma* of Christ than the Christian missionaries![54]

Too often the Church has come into contexts with a crusading mind rather than a crucified mind. But the Church only remains truly apostolic when it decides to know nothing in the world except the crucified Lord (1 Corinthians 2.2). As a result, Koyama asks, 'what does the *stigma* of Jesus Christ mean for our evangelism?'[55] But challenging the Church he states, 'I am suggesting something more than some adjustments to be made in our method of evangelism. I am stating the need for recovery and renewal of the *apostolic character of the church*.'[56] This fundamental posture towards evangelism can, I think, be detected in the 1982 WCC statement on mission and evangelism:

> Often, the primary confessors are precisely the non-publicized, unsensational people who gather together steadfastly in small caring communities, whose life prompts the question: 'What is the source of the meaning of your life? What is the power of your powerlessness?' Shared experiences reveal how often Christ is confessed in the very silence of a prison cell or of a restricted but serving, waiting, praying church. Mission calls for a serving church in every land, a church which is willing to be marked with the stigmata (nail marks) of the crucified and risen Lord. In this way the church will show that it belongs to that movement of God's love shown in Christ who went to the periphery of life.[57]

I'm almost certain that Koyama would have had a hand in crafting this statement although my half-hearted attempts to work out if that is the case have failed. Again, I don't see this posture for evangelism – the wounded hands, empty – coming up in any training manuals or conference papers.

Spat-upon and periphery evangelism

Interrelated to this, Koyama asks us to consider another Christo-logical question – the finality of Christ Jesus. 'In Jesus Christ, God came to us with his final plan, final seriousness, final demonstration of love, final sacrifice.'[58] For those of us mostly in the global north who have experienced only mild rejection for sharing the good news it is perhaps difficult to conceive of these notions of 'stigma' and 'spat-upon' evangelism. Shar-ing Jesus may have been met with mild irritation, eye rolling or bad-tempered annoyance – even outright anger – but it is unlikely to have been anything more dramatic.

Some parts of the Christian Church may wish to argue that the Christian faith is being attacked by government and society. The Labour government in the 1990s via Alastair Campbell famously said they didn't 'do God'. In an era of cancel culture there is fear around prohibiting 'conversion therapy' or people not being allowed to wear crosses at work or banning Christ-mas. We might ask how this fits with the idea of a 'spat-upon' evangelism? Are these 'persecutions' in the UK context more about a refusal to listen than bearing the stigmata? It perhaps highlights a tension in the idea of Christians as marginalized or 'spat upon' as a mark of authentically following Christ when this could just be an excuse for Christians to be objectionable perhaps?

During our five years in Cambodia, we received many visitors from the UK who were supporters, and often curious about what our life looked like. Our dear friends Brian and Debbie[59] came to spend a few days with us in the town of Neak Leoung which hugs the eastern bank of the Mekong river. Much of our time we spent taking them to visit church members from the local congregation who lived in the surrounding villages.

One particular morning we visited a family who had been Christians for some 15 years but had only seen a handful of people come to faith in Jesus from their particular village. The village was located 3 or 4 kilometres off the main road along typically dusty tracks that would be completely flooded during the rainy season. That morning we walked through the village and the rice paddies learning something of their story. Back in their modest wooden home, we acted as translator between Somnang the patriarch and Brian and Debbie. The conversation ebbed and flowed around being a follower of Jesus in Cambodia and the UK. Suddenly Somnang, quite matter of factly, as if he'd been waiting to reveal this fact, told us, 'Everyone in this village hates us.' Brian and Debbie in a typically British way were clearly uncomfortable with such an outburst, and we moved the conversation on to something less embarrassing.

Once we had arrived back at our house Brian turned to me with a look of bewilderment, possibly incredulity, and said, 'Surely they don't mean everyone hates them?' Brian found it almost impossible to imagine the level of hostility to the embodiment of Jesus that this family were in their community. This was partly because in Brian's experience of being a well-respected, white, middle-class man he had never found himself on the underside of life or pushed to the margins. He might have been mildly or even acutely embarrassed at times admitting he was a follower of Jesus, yet the positions of power he occupied meant being 'spat upon' was unlikely. Some of this kind of attitude is I think rooted in what Paas describes as a 'nostalgic idolization of Christendom'.[60] In this nostalgia, in a subtle way, God is replaced by a glorified past where Christians were secured against criticism, ridicule, suffering and persecution. In contrast, Koyama points out that the crucified Christ is just as much an important sign and witness in our evangelism as a victorious Christ.

Of course, Somnang's story is replicated across many parts of the world and there are certainly many more extreme versions of 'spat-upon' evangelism. Persecution for many Christians across the global south is a daily reality – whether Dalit Christians navigating the caste system in India, evangelical indigenous pastors in the central Asian countries of Uzbekistan and Tajikistan, or of those living and working in Islamic regimes. In their varied contexts is a uniting understanding of

sharing in the sufferings of Christ Jesus. 'Spat-upon' evangelism is not just a theory in these contexts.

American death-row inmate Mumia Abu-Jamal muses,
'Isn't it odd that Christendom – that huge body of humankind that claims spiritual descent from the Jewish carpenter
of Nazareth – claims to pray to and adore a being who was
a prisoner of Roman power, an inmate of the empire's death
row?' And yet too often the Christian Church wants to know
the power of the resurrection without a willingness to share
in the fellowship of Jesus' sufferings.[61] For many of us in the
global north the experience of following Jesus by and large
resonates with Brian's experience. Yet, as Israel Olofinjana
points out, 'Majority world Christians have lived the experience of powerlessness and weakness due to the historic context
of subjugation through enslavement and colonialism.'[62] We
need to be more attentive to those across the globe whose lived
experience of evangelism and witness is much more costly than
many of us have lived.

Slow evangelism

In my copy of Andrew Kirk's *What is Mission? Theological
Explorations* which I first read 15 years ago, I still have the
scrawlings I made in my initial perusal. Kirk explains that the
tag line 'The evangelisation of the world by 2000' captured
something of the urgency mingled with over-optimism of
many evangelists and mission organizations at the turn of a
new century. In the margin in red pen, I wrote 'three mile an
hour God'. At the time I was living in Cambodia and working
alongside some of the most godly, dedicated and hardwork-
ing people I have ever come across in Christian mission and
ministry. I couldn't doubt their sincerity and love, not only for
Cambodian people but for me and my family. But there was a
troubling undercurrent in the tag line of the organization I was
part of, OMF International. OMF International's vision is to
glorify God by the urgent evangelization of East Asia's billions.

I have no problem with the idea of evangelization, and it certainly helped to be clear about who we were trying to reach, but I always struggled with the idea of urgency. During one of our annual team conferences at the lovely resort town of Sihanoukville by the impossibly warm waters of the South China Sea, there was some debate as to whether the OMF Cambodia team should remove that word 'urgent' from our tag line. I remember vividly advocating for its removal. Being a junior member of the team, my advocacy was noted but such a decision to remove or replace the word would have to be discussed at a much higher level. Koyama's meditation 'personal freedom – two billion times', written in the mid-1970s, seems to touch on this directly. Koyama in typical fashion devises a series of questions:

> Is this 'His Work' equivalent with the evangelisation of two billion as we conceive it? Or is it something more? Are we Christians to discharge the mission as we define it or as God defines it? Is our understanding always identical to God's understanding? Does God who came in Jesus Christ speak of the urgency of mission in terms of two billion people? Is our sense of urgency identical? Is God as impatient with history as we are?[63]

The idea of urgency, for me at least, pulls us away from a fundamental attribute of *missio Dei*; namely, that ultimately this is the work of God not us. While I'm a believer of human agency in mission there is a fine line between agency in its most edifying incarnation and agency that slips into the territory of power. Urgency speaks to me of a feverish attempt to get things done, people saved, across the imagined line under severe pressure of time, which is clearly running out. Urgency in evangelism feels like we are being 'coerced into'. On the other hand, a slow evangelism recognizes our utter uselessness in a good way. It invites us to be participants in the work God is doing in drawing people to Godself.

In truth, we may celebrate those moments when people

are confronted with a profound existential crisis and make a decision, often publicly, to follow Jesus. Those folk can remember the date and time of that encounter. Others may find a journey painfully slow; stumbling, limping towards Jesus unsure exactly when they found themselves on the path or whether there was a line.

Arnold and David had been friends since meeting at sixth form college in the 1990s. Arnold was confident and utterly sure of his faith, attempting to reorganize the Christian Union at his first meeting much to the bewilderment of those in leadership. David, although only 16, was already preaching on the Methodist circuit at the village chapels near his home and spending the small offering he was given for doing so at Burger King. Like most teenagers who had grown up in the church, he began questioning his faith during his A levels. His father's extramarital affairs left him sickened and confused, a complex relationship with a beautiful girl that eventually went sour caused him more anguish, plus a growing feeling that the Christian faith was illogical. His encounter with Christians at the university Christian Union only compounded the problem. Too much self-righteousness, too many people who knew the answers to everything, and little inclusiveness! By his second year David had abandoned his faith, much to the horror of his mother and father and those who knew him as the young boy preaching on the Cornish Methodist circuit. Arnold found David's exit of faith difficult to deal with. He had always felt that their relationship was rooted in their Christian faith. David was being more antagonistic each time they met. He was dismissive, on occasions snide and smirking. Arnold was no better, on occasion being sanctimonious and self-righteous about David's relationships.

They continued to be friends but meeting only occasionally as they lived in different countries for long periods. Arnold went through sporadic periods of fervent prayer for David to turn back to faith. In their forties, they began to meet more regularly. After a particularly enjoyable meal and long conversation in a pub, Arnold felt David was softening to 'the things of God' as he liked to call them – only for David the next day to dismiss any such hope via an email. Arnold decided to simply stop treating David as an evangelistic project although he had never intended for that to be the case. He did pray but in a different way. David and Arnold spent more time together – Arnold felt their relationship was deeper, more honest and vulnerable than ever before although there was no external evidence for David being more open to God. Arnold felt it was impossible to tell where David was on the Engel scale. He'd possibly gone backwards, and yet Arnold felt entirely convinced that God was at work in David. There had been times when David was pessimistic and angry. A major redundancy had left him bewildered and confused a few years earlier and anxious about the future but David was more joyful than before, more content in himself. As a result of the redundancy David had begun a new job and seemingly found his vocation. His previous cynicism in some areas had dissolved and he was exhibiting what Arnold could see as the fruit of the Spirit. Perhaps the kingdom of God was breaking into David's life ...

My friend Steve Hollinghurst reminded me that if I think my fundamental posture towards others is saving people from hell I will do so by any means possible just as I would grab someone who was drowning and pull them into the boat. I will also believe this is 'urgent' and that listening, relationship and mutuality is a waste of time. If, however, I am looking for a person to become more of who they are and to grow as a human being in Christ, I will take time; I will not want to coerce them or hold power over them. In the story of David and Arnold it seems obvious that the evangelism and discipleship have collapsed into each other. In a modernist reading these would be divided up, mess free: evangelism, decision made, discipleship in a linear and straightforward fashion. But much of life isn't like that and people cannot be coerced into acting in certain ways.

The apparent slowness on a journey towards Jesus may be the cause of grief and distress for some of us albeit that waiting and hoping are intermingled. Yet Koyama perceptively notes that 'waiting causes us psychological irritation'. It begs the question of whether we are prepared to accompany someone on the journey towards Jesus even when we don't appear to be getting anywhere? Perhaps that accompanying journey is meant to be mutually transformative? I fear, though, that some would find that idea difficult to accept. Might we be open to the slowness as a gift? In early Celtic monasticism the term *anam-chara* was used to describe 'soul friendship' – persons who acted as confessors and spiritual guide, and spiritual guides to one another. Rooted in the lives and witness of the early desert fathers and mothers a maxim of theirs was 'Be an example and not a lawgiver'. In *anamchara* friendship, hospitality and compassion are deeply valued along with silence. In confession of sin or suffering they were only permitted to reply, 'it is just as you say'. At other times no words would suffice.

Bounded set and centre set

Another way of thinking about this is to frame it in terms of a 'bounded set' and 'centre set' approach. Steve Hollinghurst says that the problem of 'Christendom is that it has turned the notion of sudden conversion into a model of entry into the church.'[64] When the focus in evangelism becomes, as Hollinghurst says, 'the smash and grab approach' we are operating in a bounded set model. It's obvious who is in and who is out.

Paul Hiebert originally put forward this idea. He said that in the bounded set approach Christians are defined by what they are: orthodoxy (what they believe) or orthopraxy (what they practise). When there is a homogeny in group belief there is a safety inside the boundary of the bounded set. There is also a sharp distinction between Christians and non-Christians. The boundary between those who are truly Christian and those who are not is important for the bounded set and is the reason that conversion and evangelism are emphasized since the focus is about getting people across the boundary of faith.[65]

Alternatively, the centre set is defined by a centre or by the relationship of the set's members to the centre. There are two intrinsic variables that define centre set membership and distance from the centre. Objects become members of the set by relating to the centre. There are no second-class members of the set but the concern and focus is to encourage movement towards the centre.[66] While there is a difference between Christians and non-Christians, this does not become the defining feature of the set.

In an evangelism of listening, purposefully slow, and deeply concerned with the *imago Dei* and the idea of accompanying journey, the centre set approach makes sense.

Conclusion

Back to Koyama. What does the *stigma* of Jesus mean for evangelism? How do we make up for those many centuries of not listening? The years of too many words need to be balanced with a new posture of listening, silence and vulnerability. We will need to cultivate discernment as whether to speak or not to speak. We may need to consider how we live with the *stigma* of Jesus Christ in our evangelism. And we may need to be more honest about slowness or some journeying towards Jesus.

Notes

1 D. Irvin, 1996, 'The Mission of Hospitality: To Open the Universe a Little More' in D. Irvin and A. Akinade, *The Agitated Mind of God: The Theology of Kosuke Koyama*, Maryknoll, NY: Orbis Books, p. 173.

2 K. Koyama, 1979, *Three Mile an Hour God*, London: SCM Press, p. 51.

3 The objectification of human beings for the purposes of an evangelism stratagem is something that Koyama further develops in his meditation 'personal freedom – two billion times'. Koyama muses upon the church growth movement's obsession with numbers and the commodification of people as number. 'I am convinced somewhere in the depth of quality of "being human" that I, the human being, am of

greater value than even two billion pounds. The idea of two billion people comes to me in a completely different way. Immediately I sense I cannot tame them, I cannot control them, I cannot possess them.' There is a 'sacred dimension in man which defies and rejects being numbered'. K. Koyama, 1975, *50 Meditations*, Maryknoll, NY: Orbis Books, p. 182.

4 Koyama, *50 Meditations*, p. 52.

5 D. M. Thang, 2017, 'The Crucified Mind: Kosuke Koyama's Missiology of "Theology of the Cross"', *Exchange* 43(1), p. 17.

6 K. Koyama, 1980, 'The Crucified Christ Challenges Human Power' in *Your Kingdom Come: Mission Perspectives*. World Conference on Mission and Evangelism, Geneva: Commission on World Mission and Evangelism, WCC Publications, p. 162.

7 Koyama, 'The Crucified Christ Challenges Human Power', p. 161.

8 Koyama, 'The Crucified Christ Challenges Human Power', p. 163.

9 Koyama, 'The Crucified Christ Challenges Human Power', p. 163.

10 K. Koyama, 1984, *Mount Fuji and Mount Sinai: A Pilgrimage in Theology*, Maryknoll, NY: Orbis Books, p. 240.

11 Koyama, *Mount Fuji and Mount Sinai*, p. 242.

12 J. Engel, 1979, *Contemporary Christian Communication: Its Theory and Practice*, New York: Thomas Nelson.

13 S. Paas, 2019, *Pilgrims and Priests: Christian Mission in a Post-Christian Society*, London: SCM Press, p. 166.

14 K. Koyama, 1977, *No Handle on the Cross: An Asian Meditation on the Crucified Mind*, Eugene, OR: Wipf and Stock.

15 All names are anonymized throughout this chapter.

16 S. Paas, 2021, 'Missional Christian Communities in Conditions of Marginality: On Finding a "Missional Existence" in the Post-Christian West', *Mission Studies* 38(1), p. 151.

17 H. Kwiyani, 2019, 'Can the West Really be Converted?', Missio Africanus, *Journal of African Missiology* 4(1), p. 80.

18 A. Kirk, 1999, *What is Mission? Theological Explorations*, London: Darton, Longman & Todd, p. 242. David Bosch also notes this is true of the WCC and Catholics too. For a thorough and nuanced discussion on Mission as Evangelism, Bosch remains a helpful starting point, although 30 years old (D. Bosch, 1991, *Transforming Mission: Paradigm Shifts in Theology of Mission*, Maryknoll, NY: Orbis Books, pp. 409–20).

19 J. Romus, 2001, 'Evangelization in the Contemporary Roman Catholic Thought', *Indian Journal of Theology* 43(1&2), p. 8.

20 See https://sioncommunity.org.uk.

21 Pope Paul VI, 1975, *Evangelii Nuntiandi*, Vatican: Libreria Editrice Vaticana.

22 I. Bria, 1993, 'Dynamics of Mission in Liturgy', *International Review of Mission* 82(327), p. 318.

23 Bosch, *Transforming Mission*, p. 409.

24 M. Mosebach, 2019, *The 21: A Journey into the Land of the Coptic Martyrs*, Robertsbridge: Plough Publishing House.

25 P. Cruchley-Jones, 2016, 'Evangelism from the Margins: Experiences of the Ironic in Evangelism in Cardiff, UK', *International Review of Mission* 105(1), pp. 33–4.

26 B. Keith, 2017, 'Exploring Attitudes to Evangelism: An Ethnographic Study of Street Angels and Club Angels', *Anvil* 33(2), p. 7.

27 R. Warren, 1996, *Signs of Life: How Goes the Decade of Evangelism?*, London: Church House Publishing, p. 1.

28 Keith, 'Exploring Attitudes to Evangelism', p. 7.

29 Keith, 'Exploring Attitudes to Evangelism', p. 8.

30 See https://sharingjesus.life.

31 S. Paas, 'Missional Christian Communities in Conditions of Marginality', p. 146.

32 G. C. Fuimara, 1990, *The Other Side of Language: A Philosophy of Listening*, Oxford: Routledge, p. 12.

33 Fuimara, *The Other Side of Language*, p. 19.

34 S. Hedahl, 1998, 'Review of Gemma Corradi Fuimara: *The Other Side of Language: A Philosophy of Listening*', *Homiletic* 23(2), pp. 40–2.

35 Churches Together in England, 'Churches Group for Evangelisation', *Churches Together in England*, https://cte.org.uk/mission/coordin ating-groups/churches-group-for-evangelisation/, accessed 1.4.2022.

36 Pope Francis, 2013, *Evangelii gaudium*, Vatican: Libreria Editrice Vaticana, p. 22.

37 James 1.19b.

38 In M. Moynagh, 2012, *A Church in Every Context: An Introduction to Theology and Practice*, London: SCM Press, p. 294.

39 E. A. Heath, 2008, *The Mystic Way of Evangelism: A Contemplative Vision for Christian Outreach*, Ada, MI: Baker Academic, p. 125.

40 Moynagh, *A Church in Every Context*, p. 252.

41 P. Rollins, 2006, *How (Not) to Speak of God*, London: SPCK Press.

42 Koyama, 'The Crucified Christ Challenges Human Power', p. 157.

43 D. Bonhoeffer, 1997, *Letters and Papers from Prison* (ed.) Eberhard Bethge, New York: Touchstone.

44 Bonhoeffer, *Letters and Papers from Prison*, p. 279.

45 R. Williams, 2003, *Silence and Honey Cakes: The Wisdom of the Desert*, London: Lion Books, p. 70.

46 I. Novsima, 2019, 'A Nonverbal Mission: An Apophatic Missi-

ology from the Trauma Experience of Women with Intellectual Disabilities in Indonesia', *International Review of Mission* 108(1), p. 79.

47 Novsima, 'A Nonverbal Mission', p. 82.

48 Paas, 'Missional Christian Communities in Conditions of Marginality', p. 150.

49 J. Swinton, 2017, *Becoming Friends with Time: Disability, Timefullness and Gentle Discipleship*, London: SCM Press, pp. 124–7.

50 Novsima, 'A Nonverbal Mission', p. 86.

51 Koyama, *No Handle on the Cross*, p. 32.

52 Koyama, *No Handle on the Cross*, p. 38.

53 Koyama, *No Handle on the Cross*, p. 39.

54 Koyama, *No Handle on the Cross*, p. 40.

55 Koyama, *No Handle on the Cross*, p. 38.

56 Koyama, *No Handle on the Cross*, p. 40.

57 World Council of Churches (WCC), 1983, 'Mission and Evangelism – An Ecumenical Affirmation', *International Bulletin of Missionary Research* 7(2), p. 69.

58 WCC, 'Mission and Evangelism – An Ecumenical Affirmation', p. 90.

59 Names have been anonymized in this chapter.

60 Paas, Missional Christian Communities in Conditions of Marginality', p. 150.

61 Philippians 3.10.

62 I. Olofinjana, 2021, *Discipleship, Suffering and Racial Justice: Mission in a Pandemic World*, Oxford: Regnum, p. 52.

63 Koyama, *50 Meditations*, Maryknoll, NY: Orbis Books, p. 183.

64 S. Hollinghurst, 2010, *Mission Shaped Evangelism: The Gospel in Contemporary Society*, Norwich: Canterbury Press, p. 182.

65 P. Hiebert, 1994, *Anthropological Reflections on Missiological Issues*, Grand Rapids, MI: Baker Books, p. 115.

66 Hiebert, *Anthropological Reflections on Missiological Issues*, p. 122.

5

Surrendering:
Nailed Down!

Introduction

Whether at his betrayal, his trial or his crucifixion, Jesus surrendered himself to powerlessness. Yet God brought about a
mighty resurrection, which is the cornerstone of our Christian
hope. Unfortunately, the Church, at various times in its history,
has struggled with relinquishing temporal power and its leaders
time and again have given in to the temptation of embracing
it. Instead, we think we have nailed it, but are far from understanding what Koyama calls 'the "efficiency" of the crucified
one'. In this chapter I want to take a closer look at the idea
of surrender, embracing powerlessness, and the nailing down
of the crucified Christ and his subsequent immobility, all of
which were important themes in Koyama's writing.

As outlined in earlier chapters, the destruction of Tokyo,
subsequent bombings of Hiroshima and Nagasaki during
World War Two, and the idolatry of emperor worship were
such a 'root' experience for Koyama that nearly everything he
wrote and reflected on find their starting points in that series of
events in some way. The devastation and death that Koyama
witnessed bore in him profound experiences of bewilderment,
loss and acknowledgement at the utter fragility of human
beings and human culture. It is true that in just a few days after
the bombing of Hiroshima parts of the tram network were up
and running again. However, while it doesn't diminish human
beings' capacity for enormous resilience, we are still flesh and
blood, bone, marrow and sinew – fragility personified.

Koyama reflected on the human condition as learning to live with, and embrace, slowness, immobility, a tendency towards idolatry, delusions of grandeur, and ultimately being faced with our own deterioration and death. But he didn't do this in a fatalistic or defeatist way. Koyama was an advocate of the materiality of human existence – its bodily *this*ness. The necessity of embracing the material and local is the site at which Christian living and discipleship take place. Some quarters of Christianity have over-emphasized an otherworldly experience that has led to all sorts of abuses – salvation is never merely 'pie in the sky when you die'. That version of Christianity has sought to suggest that we are immortal souls and our bodies weigh us down, inhibiting us, imprisoning us. It has continued the binary of body and soul as fundamentally opposed to each other, which is often unhelpful.

This does not mean in any sense resigning ourselves to surrender in fatalistic ways but in self-conscious and life-affirming ways. We know Christ Jesus surrendered his will to the Father – he surrendered both his will, spirit and his body. Jesus continually spoke of only doing what the Father called him to do. He found his nourishment from doing the will of his Father.

In this chapter I explore the idea of surrender in mission and ministry in three quite broad and diverse ways. First, by considering Christ's nailing down and his immobility. What does surrendering to immobility mean for us as Christians? Koyama says, 'Jesus abandons himself to human dominance, even to crucifixion. This inefficient way is the secret of his power that confronts human power. It is the secret of his love.'[1] Throughout history Christians have forged some of their most powerful theology when essentially immobile. Whether Bonhoeffer in the last few months of his life in Tegel prison before his execution or Mother Julian the anchoress at Norwich in the late thirteenth century – surrendering to immobility may contain an opportunity to display the story of Jesus in new ways. I suggest that we may learn something about immobility from disability theology for the mission of the Church.

Second, we consider the 'efficiency' – and perhaps on some

level the potential idolatry – of technology. Our insatiable thirst for the virtual during the coronavirus pandemic of 2020–2 functioned as a catalyst for digital engagement like never before. It catapulted us into the future in a way perhaps no other event could have. We saw a euphoric response from some as they live-streamed their services from living rooms to the world and watched the numbers of those 'in attendance' rise to levels never anticipated or hoped for from a service in the church building. The other side of the story is darker. Loneliness and depression rose to unprecedented levels. Quite the extent of the tsunami wave of mental health problems remains to be seen as we navigate the coronavirus recovery era. There are obviously enormous benefits from enhancing the power of technology, but it is never an impartial exercise.

In 2021 it was announced that Jeff Bezos, tech overlord and the founder of Amazon, was investing significant sums in the Altos Labs, an anti-ageing company questing for eternal youth. It was another step in the pursuit of the freedom from the limitations of our bodies, which the transhumanism movement has been propagating for decades. There is also the growing influence of Artificial Intelligence (AI) in many spheres of life to such an extent that most of us are no longer aware of quite how much AI impacts and shapes us. There are continued questions around the value of social media platforms such as Facebook, Twitter and Instagram. Whistleblowers from within the industry giants are calling out big tech arrogance. Every day people are finding their self-worth, identity and value being marred, disfigured and at times crushed.

The third aspect of surrender is our self-identity as dust and ashes. Koyama writes about the power there is in finding an identity rooted in seeing ourselves as 'but dust'. Anyone who has attended a funeral will be familiar with the words 'From dust we hence came to dust we shall each return.' Doing mission in the light of the certainty of our dustiness and death may seem odd, depressing or fatalistic, but perhaps our relationship with our own finitude is in fact potentially releasing for us as the people of God into the world.

'Inefficiency' and being nailed down

Koyama worked with a the recurring theme of the 'inefficiency' of God in Christ. Koyama suggests that God chooses to work slowly and inefficiently as a way of revealing God's love. Towards the end of the narrative in the Gospels we meet a Christ resolutely walking towards his death. Koyama describes the situation like this:

> Jesus Christ came. He walked towards the 'full stop'. He lost his mobility. He was nailed down! He is not even at three miles an hour as we walk. He is not moving. 'Full stop'! What can be slower than 'full stop' – 'nailed down'? At this point of 'full stop', the apostolic church proclaims that the love of God to man is ultimately and fully revealed.[2]

As we have seen, during the initial stages of the coronavirus pandemic in March 2020 most churches were forced to close by the ecclesiastical hierarchy. The physical shutting of churches and the inability of clergy and lay people alike to move and minister brought up profound questions about where missional authority and power might be located. These events spawned a thousand blog posts, academic articles and video feeds and, later, books and webinars. It invited questions about a new era of mission and ministry in, and out of, our very woundedness and immobility.

Being subject to a stay at home order from government for everyone except those designated as key workers was perhaps painful to those of us who considered their vocation to be fundamentally important. Clergy and many of us used to playing pivotal roles in communities were faced with our own immediate uselessness. While we were encouraged to clap for carers, not being able to visit the dying and bereaved, the lonely and isolated, the afraid and bewildered – apart from a wave through a glass window – was a profound and almost unbearable loss. This is what Sam Wells notes when he says, 'There's no point telling the world how important you [church leaders] are and insisting that for you, nothing must change, even though the whole world is having to make endless adaptations.'[3]

Across the churches, whether liberal or conservative, many mourned the public act of gathering, consecrating the bread and wine, and feeding their communities and congregations. Some live-streamed these acts of grace from their kitchen tables – for which they were unfairly mocked or taken to task for domesticating the Eucharist – perhaps forgetting the early Church likely did something similar. Others peered at the screen wishing they could taste and 'see'. Some moved into action mode through supplying the needs of their local communities with food parcels, telephone calls, providing medicines, setting up a neighbourhood WhatsApp group. Whether motivated by action or numbed by a not-knowing of what to do and how to function, the severe limitations impacted all of us in different ways. But many struggled with accepting that our freedom needed to be curtailed at least for a period. By the end of the second wave of the pandemic, and the so-called Freedom Day in July 2021, the mantra of 'it's time we started getting on with our lives' was aimed at the fit and healthy only. The clinically vulnerable, the disabled, pregnant women and the elderly were sacrificed for the economy and the 'greater good'.

There is a narrative in popular culture that eschews any talk of limitations. This is not simply a libertarian position that cannot abide any intervention by government in a free economy and people's inalienable right to do whatever they wish. For some of the middle classes, accustomed to constant mobility while valorizing the home as a place of comfort and safety, there was a balk at the thought of being unable to up sticks at will.[4] There is a narrative with the view that suggests we can simply imagine our way out through the power of positive thinking. The shelves of most bookshops are weighed down by this narrative. We are told sheer acts of will enable us to overcome our limitations. While self-realization seems a good thing and affirming the agency of persons is to be lauded, how does that sit with the idea of limitation being the secret of love? If, as Koyama suggests, the apostolic Church proclaims that the love of God to human beings is ultimately and fully revealed in the immobility and 'nailed downness' of God's son, what does that potentially mean for the great missional impulse to go out into all the world and make disciples? What sense can there be in immobility and 'inefficiency' for Christian mission?

Immobility, inefficiency and mission

I wonder if the work of theologians who have reflected on disability might help us think about immobility, inefficiency and mission in fresh ways. Disability theology takes absolutely seriously the lived experiences of disabled people and invites us to reflect on how aspects of vulnerability, frailty, pain, weakness and physical and cognitive limitation may reveal new aspects of discipleship and mission. John Swinton[5] defines disability theology as 'the attempt by disabled and non-disabled Christians to understand and interpret the gospel of Jesus Christ, God, and humanity against the backdrop of the historical and contemporary experiences of people with disabilities'.[6] For Swinton, doing theology is always an embodied and interpretative enterprise. For example, we tend to think and theorize about God's power as an extension of our own power but to an unlimited degree. We are limited but God is unlimited. Disability theology subverts these assumptions by asking us to reconsider the typical narrative, inviting us to see the hermeneutic employed through most of Christian history. Swinton says that ablebodiedness has functioned as the norm and as a result has squeezed out voices and experiences of the disabled and 'other abled'. Disabled lives have been thought not to represent God's image.[7] Second, Swinton says that the Church has too often been over-influenced by the prevailing culture of the West, and especially fallen prey to the assumptions inherent in modernity. This parallels some of Koyama's key concerns. The assumptions about what is good in modernity are related to production, speed, efficiency and mobility.

When theology is evangelized by the culture of modernity it becomes deeply problematic.

Swinton argues that disability theology opens up new vistas for thinking about God and Godself in light of the experiences of disabled people, the discipline of disability studies and church practices. Swinton notes that generally there are five areas in which this has developed. I want to draw on the first and third:

1   God as disabled.
2   God as accessible.
3   God as limited.
4   God as vulnerable.
5   God as giver and receiver.[8]

First, drawing on the work of Nancy Eiesland, Swinton notes that in re-symbolizing God as disabled, Eiesland neutralizes arguments that equate disability with sinfulness. But more than that, Swinton suggests that re-imagining God as disabled allows us to see:

> God is not outside of disability trying to heal it; but deeply implicated within it. In God's very being, God shares in the experience. This identification is not simply a matter of the social location of God (God is alongside, or sympathetic towards the disabled); it is in fact an ontological statement.[9]

The third approach in the list is the idea of God as limited. Drawing on the work of Deborah Creamer, Swinton says that limits are not to be seen fundamentally as problems. Limits are neutral and universal attributes of human beings.[10] Limitations should not be seen as 'less than'. If we are made in the image of God and that includes our very obvious physical and cognitive limitations and immobilities, how does that help us understand more clearly a God who is immobile for us as the greatest act of love? Physical immobility and slow cognitive processing could be seen as a missiological gift to the Church rather than a hindrance to its activities. However, as Swinton points out, to be slow in body and mind in a hyperactive and hypercognitive society is to risk becoming subject to the type of disturbing attitudes of people like Richard Dawkins.[11]

If the task of Christian mission is to preach the whole gospel to the whole world from the whole Church, then the gifts and experiences of disabled people are central to the Church's life and witness since they offer us deeper ways of understanding the nailed-down and immobile Christ. Disabled people are not to be only recipients of mission but to be active participants in the invitational narrative of *missio Dei*. Lesslie Newbigin wrote in 1979 that the embrace of limitation and our limited witness as the body of Christ is only made richer and more hospitable when partnering with disabled people. Disabled people are 'utterly indispensable to the churches' authentic life'.[12] Those who do not fulfil the modern categories of the free autonomous self, but are instead dependent and have little power or choice, remind us of the basic posture we are called to inhabit as missionary disciples – trust, dependency and faith.

Koyama on technology and *maya*

Koyama's longest book is his 1984 *Mount Fuji and Mount Sinai*. In it he deals with idolatry, writing extensively about the Japanese context and the cult of the emperor. In many senses Koyama wrote out of this kind of psychological wound of idolatry. His pilgrimage in theology is intertwined with a meditation on idolatry. He says that what began as a vague feeling or uneasiness about the violent cult of the emperor 'became a preoccupation with the mysterious power of idolatry in history'.[13] But, says Koyama, 'idols do not come into being ambiguously'.[14] Honed out of wood or stone in the past, idolatry for Koyama is rooted in the idea that something particular or conditional is elevated as unconditional. He urges us not to fall into the trap of believing that biblical characterizations of idols and idolatry are too simplistic or static to describe the complicated social and political phenomena of our modern world. To do so on our part would be naive. While there are many potential idols in the modern world – whether ideologies like nationalism or totalitarianism – Koyama takes specific aim at technology throughout his writings. Japan in the 1970s and 1980s (despite a few wobbles) was economically robust and at the cutting edge of global technological advancement. Those of us who coveted a Sony Walkman for our cassettes know this only too well. Koyama saw the foolishness of the idolatry of the emperor at the end of the World War Two and perhaps began to suspect something potentially similar emerging in Japan's love and embrace of the technological. It brings out a confidence in our own abilities and tempts us to believe we have powers of control and mastery that nearly always lead to a fall.

Koyama perhaps foresaw the potential totalizing power that technology wrongfully promises. Somewhat prophetically he says, 'when an obsession with technology begins to represent the universal meaning of human existence, then idolatry will take place'.[15] Writing at a point in history where the proliferation of nuclear weapons was at a deeply worrying point and because of his own experience, Koyama was concerned about the arms race. In the case of skilfully made nuclear weapons, before them 'we fall down and worship', says Koyama.[16] When idols become eloquent and we are dumb before them, we can see the demonic power of idolatry.

The world's relationship with technology is all too apparent. But, more poignantly, the Church's relationship with it – with the rise of artificial intelligence, the very real possibilities of human enhancement offered by transhumanism, and our love affair with the digital – needs careful examination. Koyama was profoundly concerned about human beings' relationship with technology, although he probably could not have anticipated quite how things would develop. Koyama asked questions about 'the "efficiency" of the crucified one' and how much we can use technology without becoming a victim of it.

Essentially, Koyama was deeply concerned about the relationship between efficiency and meaning and felt that efficiency had collapsed meaning. In the 'efficiency' of the crucified one, we find technology, theology and meaning crumpled together – with technology potentially losing its power. Koyama, like other theologians, was suspicious of the promises technology made for human beings. He felt that there was an incongruity between the technological and the spiritual. He sensed that mixing up these two kinds of powers, and what he called zones, was an affront to the *holy*.[17] Although sometimes his meditations on technology are idiosyncratic and feel as if they are based on a fairly pessimistic hermeneutic, they offer valuable insights. Koyama was suspicious of what he called the straightness and efficiency of technology. Musing upon the inner workings of a Xerox machine, for example, he says from the outside it looks 'simple, problem free, neat and orderly', All we need do is press a few buttons and the miracle of copying takes place. But Koyama says that this means technology makes us outsiders.

He draws on a Buddhist term from Hindu philosophy, *maya*. *Maya* originally denoted the magic power with which a god can make human beings believe in what turns out to be an illusion.[18] Koyama argues that technology can *maya* us, and surround us with an attractive efficient world. Technology can dupe us into believing it can do more for us than is really possible. Therefore, we need to ask, 'how much technology can we use without being victimised by technological *maya*?'[19] There is, for Koyama, something deceptive about these 'streamlines' as he calls them. Technology for Koyama has the inherent danger of illusion and deception of cover up, or superficiality. And I think Koyama would have seen the digital age as essentially being hostile to what it means to be human. In response to these technological efficiencies and deceptions, God comes with the question he asked Adam and Eve in the Garden (who had covered themselves, ashamed of their nakedness), 'Where are you?'

Tech, technicity and the hyper-real

When I returned to live in the UK in early 2019, one way of acculturating back into British life was to watch TV. I discovered the series *Black Mirror* written by former *Guardian* journalist Charlie Brooker. The series, made up of a dazzling variety of dark tales, has been aptly described by Rebecca Nicholson as 'stand-alone dystopian techno parables'.[20] Ranging from feature length to just longer than 40 minutes, each is a complete story in itself set in the near future or a parallel reality dealing with our ever-complex relationship with technology. It highlights the unsettling feeling that we increasingly have less and less control over the technological and that human beings are being subsumed in some way or lost in the realm of the digital. One episode, 'Nosedive', takes on the obsession for 'likes' that we are so often seduced into by social media platforms. Another portrays a post-apocalyptic future where an indestructible techno dog will stop at nothing to hunt down and destroy the last vestige of humanity in a terrifying semi-nightmare. Each story explores the fragility and vulnerability of the human condition in the face of new tech. These narratives are so compelling to watch because we sense the nearness of them – they are both appalling and compelling viewing in equal measure.

The French cultural theorist, philosopher and sociologist Jean Baudrillard wrote about the complex relationship human beings have with technology and what he called *technicity* – by which he meant actual objects or instruments of technology. In his work *Simulation and Simulacra* he sought to show the essential rupture between modern and postmodern societies. For Baudrillard, modern societies are organized around the production and consumption of commodities, while postmodern societies are organized around *simulation* and the play of images and signs, denoting a situation in which codes, models and signs are the organizing forms of a new social order where simulation rules.[21] Baudrillard said that in a postmodern society an individual's identity is constructed by their appropriation of images and codes and this determines how they perceive and understand themselves and their relationship with others. Baudrillard also put forward the notion of the *hyperreal* in which the superabundance of images, codes and virtual experiences diminishes reality. Baudrillard called this 'an over proximity of all things'. For Baudrillard, an individual in a postmodern world becomes merely an entity influenced by media, technological experience, and the *hyperreal*. While we might see Baudrillard's analysis of postmodern technological society as rather pessimistic we nevertheless have to admit there are elements that may resonate with us. More of us are giving thought to our relationships with the technological or digital beyond fasting from Facebook or vowing not to get an Instagram account. There are live questions that continue to be faced and which Koyama was already beginning to ponder in the late 1970s.

Tech, modern life and the common good

Clearly, to write off all technological developments of the last 50 years would be a foolhardy and patently ridiculous thing to do. I have no wish to propose a reactionary Luddite movement, nor do I think Koyama would have done so. But while exploring technology as a gift we are invited also to employ a hermeneutic of suspicion towards it and to ask the question 'what does it mean to be human in the light of technological acceleration?'

The fourth industrial revolution, a term in common usage now, has fundamentally changed the way we live, work and relate to one another. In its scale, scope and complexity, it is unlike anything humankind has experienced before.[22] Schwab notes that this new era is differentiated from the third industrial revolution by three distinctives:

Velocity: The evolving pace is exponential rather than linear and it is because of the multifaceted and deeply interconnected world we live in. *Breadth and depth*: A factor that builds on the digital revolution and combines multiple technologies that are leading to unprecedented paradigm shifts in the economy, business, society and individually. It is not only the 'what' and 'how' that are changing but also the 'who' we are. *Systems impact*: It is about the transformation of entire systems across and within countries, companies, industries and the society as a whole.[23]

Koyama, I'm sure, had his eye on the exponential pace of technological change, and not only the pace but the very real possibility of the way in which technology could impact the 'who' of who we are – seemingly impacting the ontological. It's important not to be naive. The Church has historically had a difficult relationship with science and technological development. It viewed such advancement more as an attempt to usurp its hegemonic power over the minds and lives of its followers. On one level technological developments throughout history have given us drugs and vaccines that have utterly transformed public health in many parts of the globe. On a morning walk with my four-year-old we overheard a group of women discussing their health. 'I think I need my knees done, … you know, I had both hips replaced in 2018 …' The other women nodded in empathetic agreement. Medical technology is an everyday reality. More recently it has given us neuroprosthetics, which brings together neuroscience and biomedical engineering – for example, creating a cochlear implant and returning partial hearing to someone with profound deafness. We know that technology and technological advancement can be harnessed for the common good, bringing pain relief and new beginnings for some. And yet we fear that there is a more nefarious side to the story: the growing and disturbing movement of transhumanism or post humanism. Elaine Graham says, 'opinions polarise around whether it is appropriate to dream of transcending the frailties of the flesh to embrace new physical forms, or whether the end of our embodiment would fatally compromise our essential humanity'.[24]

'I want to live for ever!' Theological anthropology and transhumanism

As a seven-year-old I fell under the spell of the television series *Fame* – it was largely based on the leg warmers and the theme tune. Like many others, I danced round the living room with my sweatbands and hairbrush in hand as a fake mic. The theme tune was a piece of early 1980s discotech rock pop in which Irene Cara declares in the chorus, '[Fame] I'm gonna live forever, I'm gonna learn how to fly [high]'. Surely a cry for immortality.

Our human condition suggests we have some kind of longing for eternity. The writer of Ecclesiastes suggests that God has set eternity in our hearts. We want to live for ever. We want to be like God. There are themes of deification in Scripture. The author of 2 Peter writes that God in Christ has 'given us his very great and precious promises, so that through them you may participate in the divine nature'.[25] In the incarnation of Christ we see the transformation of human nature into divine (although I'm aware of the theological and doctrinal fissures in that statement). We are to be co-heirs with Christ in the future reign of God. In Orthodox theology

> ... the human person is called into a development, evolution, from being the image of the triune God, to becoming a like-ness of the Original Image. Orthodox theology names *theosis* or divinization. On her or his mission to this goal of perfec-tion, as the prophet of creation, the human person is bringing along the whole creation to its refinement.[26]

These themes of deification and our innate creativity that are rooted in the Christian tradition have some overlap with the advancement of technology in the late twentieth century. How we regard these technologies should never be an unreflective process. Elaine Graham reminds us that we should not simply regard technologies as benign tools for human self-actualization. Transhumanism regards technology as a way of bypassing the limitations of the human condition. The Transhumanist Manifesto challenges the issue of human ageing and the finality of death by advocating three conditions. These conditions assert that ageing is a disease, augmentation and enhancement to the human body and brain are essential for survival, and that human life is not restricted to any one form or environment.[27]

Transhumanists are typical children of the Enlightenment; they are firmly rooted in the notion of endless progress. They believe in individual autonomy and the possibility of transcending the limitations of tradition, superstition and fear. Whereas at one point the promises of sophisticated body modification seemed a way off, they are, and will be, increasing in availability. Whether implants into or under the skin, or more innovative implants into our brains linked with nanotechnologies, these push the boundaries around the 'who' of being human as they seek new forms of humanity. Transhumanists fundamentally believe that the merging of flesh and bone bodies with machines has the potential to create new ways of being human. The Transhumanist Manifesto moves out further from accepting ourselves as we are and towards a more complex process of physical deification, and feels particularly Babel-like when we remember God's response in Genesis 11.

Theologians such as Karen O'Donnell, formerly from the Centre for Digital Theology in Durham, seem to approach these topics with considerably less scepticism than I can employ. And I appreciate the way in which Karen has positioned herself as a theological dreamer performing thought experiments.[28] O'Donnell says quite frankly that she lays her cards on the table by arguing that *imago Dei* is not normative and set but performative. Since that is the case she suggests that there is potential in the realm of transhumanism and AI to learn, grow and develop in ways that mirror human relationality. She asks, 'if Artificial Intelligence is autonomous and can learn, as a new Christian does, to perform the image of God and seek it in the other in specific, concrete situations, then would such AI be in the image of God by virtue of performing the image? Could it be "saved"?'[29]

While I recognize the excellent postulations of O'Donnell and the questions are important, I find them somewhat utopian in nature. I want to suggest three ways (although there are doubtless more) that transhumanism is potentially unhelpful. First, if transhumanism collapses meaning into 'efficiency', which I believe it has a tendency to do, then it can be seen as a commodifying movement. Elaine Graham says that 'transhumanism exhibits a secular scepticism towards theologically grounded values'.[30] Indeed, transhumanism views the human being ultimately as a human body. The body has attributes that are merely commodities. The body may be upgraded as I upgrade my phone on my Tesco mobile contract. The body, however, is not merely an instrument, and neither does transhumanism seem to give a clear account of human beings in relation to one another.

Second, transhumanism is essentially elitist. Any quick glance through the websites of biohackers and grinders makes it obvious that this is purely for those who can afford it. The rise of transhumanism has the potential to further extenuate the gross inequalities we see being played out globally. Upgrading is and will continue to be only accessible to a few – those with enormous wealth. Whatever future projections there are for more accessible and egalitarian options, it will still be a technology that is totally unavailable to some 99 per cent of the global population.

Third, transhumanism promises a false horizon of human invincibility and freedom from pain and suffering. Whether the dreams of Jeff Bezos to create some elixir of life and inhabit eternal youth are actually possible is secondary. Transhumanism is predicated on a fundamental misstep: deification is the life of the age to come – a gift of God that cannot be realized through our own volition.

Being truly human is profoundly rooted in our physical limitations, idiosyncrasies, vulnerability, fragility and weakness. For all our longings to be freed in some way from those limitations we are living in, with and through them in our physical bodies, they make us who we are called to be. This is not to write off medical technological advances in ways that are mindful of the human being, but it does call us to live honestly with the fact that we cannot ultimately avoid our frailties and finally our deaths.

'Christianity,' says Rowan Williams, 'has particular theological reason for valuing the local and material.'[31] Indeed, the incarnation is absolutely vital to reflections on our own humanity. Jesus comes to us limited and time bound, and while his resurrection body gives us a taste of our bodies' eschatological transformation it is a gift of God rather than for our own determination. We cannot engineer ourselves out of our ultimate vulnerability. As Andrew Third reminds us:

> Transhumanist suggestions that human destiny and purpose is about striving to improve and replace a frail material body to gain immortality must be challenged as simplistic and inaccurate by those who believe that humanity's past, present, and future identities are as embodied and spiritual creatures that are part of a creation that God declared 'very good'.[32]

John Swinton reminds us 'who we *truly* are – is not a product of human possibilities but is, rather, something that is given to us and at the same time hidden from us in Christ.'[33] Pressing into understanding this truth is an important consideration for Christians.

Digital church and real presence

In one of the many Zoom conversations I was invited to be part of during the pandemic lockdown, I was in a breakout room with a number of clergy, mostly of Anglo Catholic persuasion. In a discussion on technology and how church leaders had generally coped, one senior incumbent named Richard, who was clearly longing to be back in his parish church building, started proceedings with 'everything about the digital is hostile to what it means to be human!' I was struck by this comment.

Not that I agreed with it, but it was clearly born out of the pain of being isolated from the physical building he felt most at home in and where he felt most able to exercise his ministry.

Digital church is not a new concept, but Christians became aware of the possibilities in a heightened way during the coronavirus pandemic. The dramatic announcement by the UK government to ban mass gatherings on 16 March 2020, and the more radical step of banning gatherings of more than two people from different households on 23 March, threw many churches into disarray. Most church leaders commanded their clergy to lock the doors and were barred from using the church – even for personal prayer. They had to engage with the digital sphere in a way they had not needed to before. Although there were churches streaming services before the pandemic, huge numbers attempted to hold some kind of service via Zoom or streaming in the first few weeks of the lockdown. There were deep theological concerns from some quarters of the Church as is evidenced by the cry of despair from Richard. In April 2020 Pope Francis stated that 'the Church, the Sacraments, the People of God are concrete'. The idea of a virtual community of disciples connected via fibre optics was clearly problematic for many. If Koyama was reminding his readers of the potential pitfalls of technology, how do we think through the questions that are raised by digital church and real presence?

Real presence: online communion?

Back in 2009 Baptist theologian Paul Fiddes was musing on some interesting questions about virtual communion in the context of the Anglican cathedral in the online game *Second Life*.[34]

In a paper, Fiddes suggested that in a virtual world like *Second Life* where avatars worship God and avatars minister to avatars there is the possibility that the mediation of grace can happen through the materials of that world – that is, through digital representations.[35] Fiddes argues that this is never totally

virtual as those behind an avatar are involved in physically tap-
ping their keyboards or controlling a mouse, and if 'all things
live and move and have their being' this should include the
beings of virtual worlds. The need to live-stream sacraments
and worship during the pandemic brought into the frame questions about the physicality of the Eucharist and whether the
Holy Spirit can minister a gift of grace via the internet, across
screens and via pixels, silicon and photons.

The live-streaming of worship and the sacraments seemed
to elicit a number of responses. First, there were those with a
looser understanding about what is permissible who enjoyed
watching their pastor or minister celebrating communion in
his or her dining room. It gave a comfort and domesticity that
echoed the simplicity of the early Church. Generally, these
churches were Pentecostal and Charismatic churches who were
more likely to emphasis the priesthood of all believers and the
Spirit's power. In these examples, online worshippers were
encouraged to bring their own bread and wine.

Second, some priests chose to abstain from celebrating the
Eucharist as an act of solidarity with their congregation who
were deprived from receiving the bread and wine. Third, there
were those encouraged to part take in an act of spiritual communion. The Catholic Bishops' Conference of England and
Wales published a prayer from Alphonsus Ligouri a month into
the first lockdown to help church members: 'Since I cannot at
this moment receive You sacramentally, come spiritually into
my heart.'[36]

Fourth, Catholic theologian Gemma Simmonds notes that
'for others it opened up yawning chasms of interpretation with
regard to the unique nature of the sacraments, diminishing the
ultimate holiness of the sacred into everyday banality in a way
that bordered on the blasphemous. If Jesus is truly present in
the bread and wine transformed into his body and blood at
the Eucharist, what difference does it make when we are no
longer able to participate physically in this holiest and most
transformative of rituals?[37]

Real presence: who is excluded?

One of the incidental questions that the move to online services provided was around the issue of inclusion. When I was a vicar in South Africa a number of people who loved the church and would have dearly liked to have attended regularly were unable to come because they couldn't access a disabled toilet and our finances were such that we weren't able to provide one. It was a cause of great pain for some. Those who previously found physical accessibility into a church building almost impossible took delight in being able to gather each week via Zoom church. Genuine virtual participation rose – where church leaders allowed it – and there seemed to be the potential for a more egalitarian future. When so-called 'freedom day' came in July 2021 many who had been previously excluded begged their churches not to stop the virtual online element of their gathered life. This is a justice issue where those who are disabled, shielding because of a physical issue such as being immune compromised, and the elderly, potentially get overlooked as the church moves back to normal.

There were seemingly opposing attitudes from clergy and ministers towards their elderly congregants. Some suggested it was a waste of time to stream services when their elderly congregants were technologically inept. Others found that by creating online services their older members in fact learnt the basic skills to work their iPads sufficiently and greatly enjoyed being together.

Considering how virtual church builds relational capital, allows those previously excluded to truly find a place in the community, and sustains a more democratic approach to ecclesial life is key. While digital church has allowed those previously excluded from entering into a building to be present, there is also the question of digital poverty – there are estimated to be around two million people in the UK who still have no access.

Real presence: missiological questions

Early research in the first five to six months of the pandemic suggested that thousands were tuning into church services on Facebook live, YouTube and other platforms as a 'taster'; some people saw this as an unequalled missional opportunity and there were pleas to consider hybrid church (in the building and online) as the 'new normal'. Alexander Chow and Jonas Kurlberg certainly suggest that '... digital technologies offer new possibilities for the expression of the church's missional role, beyond the limits of space and geography. But it is not only a matter of the utility of digital technologies. Digital technologies raise questions of how the church's mission needs to adapt to the ever-changing realities of the present.'[38]

While giving people an opportunity to 'see' what church is like before having to cross the physical threshold of walking through the door, Australian missiologist Mike Frost, in the early stages of the pandemic, saw the 'counting' of viewing numbers as a fatal flaw. Frost argues that the lure of seeing numbers skyrocket of the people in 'attendance' means the consumerist mentality of church shopping makes it like Uber-Eats. Frost says, 'the spike in online attendance will be as illusory as the growth of megachurches last century. It will serve to mask the reality that less and less people are devoted to a wholehearted commitment to Christ.'[39] I think this was probably a premature response to some degree – Chow and Kurlberg narrate the story at Durham Cathedral:

> At Durham Cathedral, the high interest in their live-streamed services and daily prayer has caught the clergy by surprise. Charlie Allen is baffled by the thousands of viewers joining their daily prayers compared to the twenty-odd persons they normally have in the cathedral. Their viewers are geographically dispersed, and they are considering creating local groups in order to connect these individuals for mutual support.[40]

Indeed, there are initiatives that have taken very seriously the potential to create, nurture and sustain long-term virtual church communities that are rooted in the rhythms of the daily offices. The London Internet Church[41] has been in existence since 2010 although it has most recently returned to the website of its mother church, St Stephen Walbrook, in the city of London. With opportunities to light virtual candles, take part in daily prayers, and email through requests for prayer, the idea of it promoting a consumerist attitude towards church life rings a little hollow.

Since 2019 I've been a trustee for the Christian Enquiry Agency, the small charity behind the website www.christianity. org.uk. Our aim is to be a safe, balanced and impartial virtual space where people can explore the Christian faith through a number of excellent articles written from an ecumenical perspective. Every week we receive many emails asking all sorts of questions about faith, requesting prayer, and asking advice on what church to join in a local area. I have been struck by the very raw and real questions that are asked and the candid nature of what people share about themselves and their journey. Often these are folk who have been badly hurt by the Church in the past. The website offers an anonymity that is vital for many people in the early explorations of faith.

Clearly, Koyama had concerns about technology and its ability to *maya* us, and these should continue to be taken seriously in our assessment of technological advancements. Technology's double edge – as both a gift and a potential curse – needs to be considered carefully. The ability to offer promised connectivity on the one hand only tells a partial story. The web of disinformation in conspiracy theories and the like will continue to be a threat to human flourishing. Many of us know the pain and discord sown on social media platforms in personal spats. Some people involved in needless #Anglicantwitter warfare might do well to consider signing up to the Digital Charter.[42] Our propensity for publicly wounding one another is tragic.

More complex areas like AI, human augmentation and transhumanism for me have so much potential to warp our notions of being human. While I acknowledge that technology is advancing at a pace and far quicker than I might assume, the possibility of damaging us as human beings frightens me.

Dust and ashes: our self-identity[43]

At the period in the church calendar known as Lent, we are actively encouraged to remember that we are dust and to dust we shall return. Our dustiness is not something many of us wish to contemplate any longer than is necessary, Ash Wednesday and funeral services withstanding. But in this long-range meditation on surrender, dust and ashes as our self-identity may be more central to our ministry and mission than we care to admit.

In one of Koyama's typical meditations on Scripture he wonders aloud what was happening in the story of Abraham when he was pleading and bargaining with God for the lives of a handful of righteous people in the city of Sodom in Genesis 18. Koyama argues that in his pleading with God over the people of Sodom, Abraham never forgets his dust and ashes identity. 'Between the holy God and the unholy city stood Abraham who felt himself but dust and ashes.'[44] The surrender to our earthiness that Koyama suggests is actually the root of both spiritual and political power. When we recognize our limitations in ability and capacity for holiness we live in a place of creativity. Strangely, notes Koyama, it is Abraham's self-identity as dust and ashes that 'provided him with spiritual, psychological and intellectual energy to wrestle with problems.'[45] When we embrace this identity – live in surrender – we cannot be threatened; we are fearless and free and can live for others. In dust and ashes identity we are proclaiming on some level or another our irrelevance. As Henri Nouwen says, we need more people 'who dare to claim their irrelevance in the contemporary world as a divine vocation that allows them to enter into deep solidarity with the anguish underlying all the glitter of success, and to bring the light of Jesus there.'[46]

Increased wealth, prosperity and the astonishing advances in technology have fooled many of us into believing we are somehow immune from pain and death. Some of us want to rail against the seeming injustice of being a frail human being. As set out earlier, in the global north we have largely pushed death to the outskirts of our existence, but surrender is about coming to terms with our own limitations, vulnerability and weakness. In short, living in a way that makes us face the possibility of death is not necessarily a bad thing. The pandemic forced us to consider that any of us may die 'before our time'. Tragically, two of my wife's cousins, aged 33 and 35, died of Covid on separate continents just a few months apart. That narrative was echoed across the globe.

Hiromasa Mase says that 'in an age in which life can be manipulated, our interest in protecting life grows stronger. But since death is the reverse side of life, why should we not talk about death without hesitation as part of life?'[47] Clearly, there are central themes around death and life and resurrection in Jesus' teaching in the New Testament. In John 12.24 Jesus highlights the principle that death is essential to further life. Unless a grain of wheat falls to the ground and dies it remains alone, but if it dies it bears much fruit. To follow Jesus is to give up self-assertion and self-seeking and die to self and its ego. Ego death is central to discipleship. This is an essential truth, but I want to suggest it is more than a metaphor. Richard Rohr helps me see the link between facing actual physical death as a vital part of living what he calls the second half of life. 'Most of nature seems to totally accept major loss, gross inefficiency, mass extinctions and short life spans as the price of life at all.'[48]

How do we face death?

Our relationship to death, our own and that of others, reveals something of our way of being in the world. Two funeral stories from my time as a priest in South Africa exemplify two distinct responses to death. The first concerns an English heritage white family from an upper-middle-class suburb in a large city. I received a telephone call one morning to say that the father, in his late fifties, had died the previous day after a short but painful battle with cancer. The family were not connected to the church in any way. As might be imagined, his wife and two children in their twenties were devastated – bereft. In the phone call it was clear they wanted to sort out details quickly and precisely. 'We don't want the body in the church,' they told me. 'We don't want to see him.' The unbearable thought of having to see their beloved sealed in a coffin was too much. The local bishop had put a moratorium on having no coffin in the church, so I gently suggested to the family that it would be much better for emotional closure if the coffin were present. I don't recall the final decision made but envisaging the body, even sealed in its fine oak veneer coffin, was psychologically and emotionally devastating for the family. Death was some-thing that happened to other people. On one level this is of course understandable but perhaps not helpful. We can insu-late ourselves from much pain and suffering but we all have to surrender to death – when we pretend it's a sort of slipping into the next room, ethereal, bodiless and silent, we deceive ourselves entirely.

The second story recalls the death of a young Burundian man who had joined our congregation in Cape Town. Joseph, like many others, had escaped the civil war that began in 1993. He had travelled overland and had eventually reached Cape Town in 2006. The xenophobic riots in townships that took place across South Africa in 2008 saw Joseph and a number of others taking refuge in the church hall. He and his family then settled in the congregation, learning English and taking an active part in services. Joseph eventually found work riding a motorbike delivering medicines for a local chain of pharmacies. Tragically, one afternoon Joseph was killed instantly in a head-on collision with a lorry. His death was a blow to the community. He left behind a beautiful wife who was pregnant and a small son.

The funeral, on a typically wet sideways-rain Cape Town afternoon, was loud and boisterous. The coffin arrived at the back of the church several hours before – an open casket as requested. They wanted to see the body. The community wanted to verify it really was Joseph. Without the body it would have been a farce for them. As the mourners flowed into the back of the building many touched or kissed him or gently wept over him. They spoke to him. Put a hand on his chest as they conversed together, lurching between sobs and laughing in what seemed like seconds.

The service began following the typical Anglican order I had taken many times before. At an appropriate point, a photo montage of Joseph was projected on to a large screen at the front of the church. The next moment I have indelibly fixed in my memory. Amani, Joseph's wife, let out a scream of loss and despair from the core of her being which filled every corner of the building as she collapsed from the front pew on to her knees. A few women came to support her but didn't rush her to her feet. Joseph was dead and the grief of that loss was all too apparent.

We all live, as Kelsey puts it, on 'borrowed breath' that is God's gift to give and withdraw.[49] For many of us in the global north our affluence and relative peace has shielded us from death. Yet 'only as beings inseparable from death do people have an authentic way of living'.[50] The coronavirus pandemic in the global north context was in many ways a wake-up call to the closeness of death that much of sub-Saharan Africa lives with on a daily basis. The insecurity and fragility of life. Yet I am in no way lauding that or making light of how prevalent 'dying before your time' is.

In Japanese culture Basho, the *haiku* poet, when asked by his disciples to write his final *haiku* on his deathbed, said that he would not write it since he had always written every *haiku* as if it would be his last. Living like this, with a heightened appreciation of life because the fact of death has been honestly faced, deserves to be called 'living to the fullest'.[51]

Living in our 'dust and ashes' identity we are called to inhabit the eternal present. Living in our dust and ashes identity we can throw off the ego and its continual pull for prestige, power and popularity, and instead 'be' for others as Jesus was a man for others. For Karl Rahner, dying with Christ is the act of Christian discipleship and also the highest consummation of human existence. So, when we gently remind ourselves of our limitations, we remember that only that which is limited and dies grows in value and appreciation.

I am 46. I experience time in a different way to my four-year-old daughter. Her days are long, extravagantly so. My days, on the basis of all the days that have passed me by, I experience as shorter. I perceive time as running out but not in a bad anxiety-inducing way. When I face my own death, when I am held by the hard contours of limitation and frailty that my years on earth inevitably will be, I can live in a new way. Free to be for others and with others.

Notes

1 K. Koyama, 1980, 'The Crucified Christ Challenges Human Power' in *Your Kingdom Come: Mission Perspectives – Report on the World Conference of Mission and Evangelism*, Geneva: World Council of Churches, p. 157.

2 K. Koyama, 1979, *Three Mile an Hour God*, Maryknoll, NY: Orbis Books, p. 7.

3 S. Wells, 2022, 'What Has the Spirit Been Saying to the Churches? ChurchWorks Commission for Covid Recovery', unpublished paper presented 11 January 2022.

4 L. Hanley, 2020, 'Lockdown has laid bare Britain's class divide', *The Guardian*, 7 April, https://amp.theguardian.com/commentisfree/2020/apr/07/lockdown-britain-victorian-class-divide, accessed 1.4.2022.

5 I draw on John Swinton's work in this chapter because of his particular writing around the relationship between timefullness, speed and disability, but Nancy Eiesland, Brian Brock, Stanley Hauerwas and Amos Yong are also helpful guides.

6 J. Swinton, 2010, 'Who Is the God We Worship? Theologies of Disability; Challenges and New Possibilities', *International Journal of Practical Theology* 14, p. 274.

7 Swinton, 'Who Is the God We Worship?', p. 277.

8 Swinton, 'Who Is the God We Worship?', p. 281.

9 Swinton, 'Who Is the God We Worship?', p. 283.

10 Swinton, 'Who Is the God We Worship?', p. 290.

11 J. Swinton, 2017, *Becoming Friends of Time: Disability, Timefull-ness and Gentle Discipleship*, London: SCM Press, p. 88.

12 L. Newbigin, 1979, 'Not Whole without the Handicapped' in G. Müller-Fahrenholz (ed.), *Partners in Life: The Handicapped and the Church*, Geneva: WCC Publications, p. 24.

13 K. Koyama, 1984, *Mount Fuji and Mount Sinai: A Pilgrimage in Theology*, London: SCM Press, p. 3.

14 Koyama, *Mount Fuji and Mount Sinai*, p. 37.

15 Koyama, *Mount Fuji and Mount Sinai*, p. 38.

16 Koyama, *Mount Fuji and Mount Sinai*, p. 38.

17 Koyama, *Three Mile an Hour God*, p. 23.

18 The Editors of Encyclopaedia Britannica, 'Maya', *Britannica*, https://www.britannica.com/topic/maya-Indian-philosophy, accessed 4.4.2022.

19 Koyama, *Three Mile an Hour God*, p. 31.

20 R. Nicholson, 2019, 'Miley Cyrus, taking back control of her distorted image in Black Mirror', *The Guardian*, 8 June, https://www.theguardian.com/commentisfree/2019/jun/08/miley-cyrus-taking-back-control-of-her-distorted-reflections, accessed 4.4.2022.

21 J. Baudrillard, 1994, *Simulacra and Simulation*, Ann Arbor, MI: University of Michigan Press, p. 3.

22 K. Schwab, 2016, *The Fourth Industrial Revolution*, London: Penguin Random House, p. 1.

23 Schwab, *The Fourth Industrial Revolution*, p. 3.

24 E. Graham, 2009, *Word Made Flesh: Writings in Pastoral and Practical Theology*, London: SCM Press, p. 312.

25 2 Peter 1.4.

26 M. Jaksic, 2021, 'Mission and Evangelism: An Orthodox Christian View' in *Sharing and Learning: The Bible, Mission and Receptive Ecumenism*, Geneva: WCC Publications, p. 96.

27 N. Vita-More, 2020, 'Transhumanist Manifesto', *Natasha Vita-More Phd*, https://natashavita-more.com/transhumanist-manifesto/, accessed 4.4.2022.

28 K. O'Donnell, 2021, 'The Theologian as Dreamer: On Theological Imagination and Human Enhancement', *Theology* 124(5).

29 K. O'Donnell, 2018, 'Performing the Imago Dei: Human Enhancement, Artificial Intelligence and Operative Image Bearing', *International Journal for the Study of the Christian Church* 18(1), p. 11.

30 Graham, 2009, *Word Made Flesh*, p. 315.

31 R. Williams, 2003, *Silence and Honey Cakes: The Wisdom of the Desert*, London: Lion Books, p. 93.

32 A. Third, 2020, 'Identity and mission in a technological future: a critical discussion of how distinctively Christian understandings of

human identity and purpose provide the foundation for a missional response to Western secular visions of the human future in light of advancing technologies', unpublished MA thesis, University of Manchester, p. 32.

33 Swinton, *Becoming Friends of Time*, London: SCM Press, p. 208.

34 Second Life is a real-time online multimedia platform that allows people to create an avatar and have an immersive experience.

35 S. Fiddes, 2009, 'Paul Fiddes – Sacraments in a Virtual World', *Me Liturgy, You Drains ...*, https://www.frsimon.uk/paul-fiddes-sacraments-in-a-virtual-world/, accessed 4.4.2022.

36 The Catholic Church, 2020, 'Spiritual Communion', *The Catholic Church*, 23 April, https://www.cbcew.org.uk/home/our-work/health-social-care/coronavirus-guidelines/prayer-and-worship-at-home/spiritual-communion-prayer-of-st-alphonsus/, accessed 4.4.2022.

37 G. Simmonds, 2022, 'The Post-Covid Theology Project', *Churches Together in England*, https://cte.org.uk/app/uploads/2022/02/RC1144-PCTP-BeingHuman_RealPresence_V2.pdf.

38 A. Chow, and J. Kurlberg, 2020, 'Two or Three Gathered Online: Asian and European Responses to COVID 19 and the Digital Church', *Studies in World Christianity* 26(3), p. 313.

39 M. Frost, 2020, 'Coronavirus could set the church back 25 years', *Mike Frost*, 14 April, https://mikefrost.net/coronavirus-could-set-the-church-back-25-years/, accessed 4.4.2022.

40 Chow and Kurlberg, 'Two or Three Gathered Online', p. 311.

41 See https://ststephenwalbrook.net/internet-church/.

42 Church of England, 'Digital Charter', *Church of England*, https://www.churchofengland.org/resources/digital-charter, accessed 4.4.2022.

43 Koyama, *Three Mile an Hour God*, p. 130.

44 Koyama, *Three Mile an Hour God*, p. 131.

45 Koyama, *Three Mile an Hour God*, p. 131.

46 H. Nouwen, 1989, *In the Name of Jesus: Reflections on Christian Leadership*, New York: Crossroad, p. 35.

47 H. Mase, 1985, 'Death and Dying: Towards an Ethic of Death', *Currents in Theology and Mission*, 12(2), p. 70.

48 R. Rohr, 2012, *Falling Upwards*, London: SPCK, p. 77.

49 D. Kelsey, 2009, *Eccentric Existence: A Theological Anthropology* (2 vols), Louisville, KY: Westminster John Knox Press.

50 Mase, 'Death and Dying', p. 70.

51 Mase, 'Death and Dying', p. 71.

6

Conclusion:
In Him All Things Hold Together

Through the last five chapters I have tried to present some of what I think are Koyama's central ideas and bring them into trialogue with my own experiences and the work of other theologians from across the globe. As I reflect on these chapters, it occurs to me how these themes are continually rooted in the person of Jesus Christ and his life, death and resurrection. In the first chapter I suggested that Koyama was truly a 'pan Christian' who resisted being shoehorned into one particular theological space. He was utterly committed to Scripture yet allowed context to bring new understanding and insight to the text. He was both orthodox and utterly open. One of my former college lecturers used to use the aphorism 'Roots down, walls down' – that sums up Koyama for me. He called out the idolatry of his own nation and yet also saw the Church capitulating to modernity's love for speed, power, efficiency and success.

In his theology Koyama was often trying to navigate a route through two seemingly dichotomous positions or playing with the paradoxes that were always surfacing in Jesus' life. Jesus is the centre person who moves to the periphery. He is the one in whom God is manifest most evidently and is yet 'inefficiency' incarnate. As far back as the late 1960s Koyama was drawing out these themes. In his first article in the *Southeast Asian Journal of Theology* as editor he wrote a brilliant reflection on 'In Him All Things Hold Together' from Colossians 1. The entire body of Koyama's writings returns again and again to the idea of 'Crucified yet ...' It is what Koyama refers to as 'the summit of the paradox of God's glory in the act of holding all things together in Jesus Christ'.[1]

I can still remember working my way through Lesslie Newbigin's autobiography in the winter of 2014 in Cape Town. As a family we spent one weekend at a beautiful house in Simon's Town overlooking False Bay. I was celebrating my first year at St John's and still desperately trying to work out what I was doing. The final page of Newbigin's autobiography takes him back from his global ecumenical journey to South Wales where he first became a Christian. As the sun rose behind the Hollandberge range to the west that morning, I read these words:

> I still see the cross of Jesus as the one place in all the history of human culture where there is a final dealing with the ultimate mysteries of sin and forgiveness, of bondage and freedom, of conflict and peace, of death and life. Although there is so much that is puzzling, so much I simply do not understand, I find here a point from which one can take one's bearing.[2]

I think Koyama would have very much found resonance with Newbigin's mysterious vision of Christ. In part, the mystery may be set out like this. Koyama explains that we are pressed by two realities. On the one hand, the reality that all things are 'held together in him' and, on the other, the reality that all things are confounded, scattered and sick. As Christians, then, we must be aware not to slip into triumphalism or be crushed by despair. Koyama says that 'it is immensely and incomparably difficult to stake one's life on a man who was crucified between two thieves outside the gate of Jerusalem trusting him to be the Lord in whom alone God's final restoration of all things was effected'.[3] Koyama asks if Christians can bear witness to Christ's crucified Lordship unless they themselves are really stumbling at it. No one, Koyama argues, is permitted to graduate from living in the tension of stumbling and triumphing trust.[4] It's the call of Christians in their sensitivity to the needs of the world to be in a state of stumbling, baptized and Christologically fertilized.[5]

Where rationalism and efficiency are taken to be the highest values in Western society we run into serious trouble. Where those traits are transferred into the language and posture of the Church there is potential for us to be thrown off course from the Church's *raison d'être*. Where we mourn the Church's loss of power and prestige, lamenting the place we once held at the centre, we can reorient ourselves in the margins where we find our true lives as the people of God. So how do we walk this tightrope, balancing our stumbling with triumphant trust?

I hope it has become obvious that Koyama saw the cross and the person of Jesus Christ as central to his own theology and his pursuit of ecumenical engagement. While playing a central role in the ecumenical movement of the World Council of Churches for several decades, Koyama was also critical of its weaknesses. He felt 'often ecumenism is located at the centre and not at the periphery. When ecumenism neglects "Jesus Christ crucified outside the city gate", it forgets the mystery of the healing authority established on the periphery of history and humanity.'[6] Ecumenism that isn't rooted in the person of Christ crucified loses its vitality and vibrancy.

In the remainder of this short chapter I want to restate some of the key themes that I think have emerged over the preceding chapters, and root them again in the centrality of Jesus the 'inefficient' one who inhabits the periphery for our sake: at each stage, I offer questions to consider.

Walking: being slower and finding grace in 'inefficiency'

Obviously the main theme of this book focuses on slowness. At the heart of his work, Koyama draws us in with the profound question, 'Is not the biblical God an "inefficient" and "slow" God because he is the God of the covenant relationship motivated by love?'[7] Since God is motivated out of covenant love, God is willing to take time in being with us. Over years and decades God works with us, in us, through us (and at times against us), shaping us slowly, painfully, gently; graciously, bizarrely and sometimes in bemusing ways. Like the course of a river flowing through the landscape, smoothing the jagged contours of our lives through God's grace. God worked with, through and against the community of Israel in the Old Testament. In many ways, Jesus Christ is 'inefficiency incarnate'. While Jewish expectation in first-century Palestine of the coming kingdom was rooted in some kind of military intervention, shock and awe tactics that would result in regime change from Rome to the Jewish spiritual elite, Jesus comes as Jewish sage. Born in a backwater of the vast Roman empire, only able to afford the lowest upon presentation in the temple,[8] on the run into Egypt as refugee Jesus is 'inefficiency incarnate' and our model for ministry and mission.

Koyama says that there is a fundamental juxtaposition in the relationship between 'being efficient' (fast) and 'being human' (slow). When human beings are continually pushed and coerced into ways of living and being that are rooted in speed and efficiency, we are in danger of losing precious dimensions of our humanity. When human beings are increasingly valued for their ability to get certain things done in certain timeframes, our humanity is degraded. To be slow is counterintuitive for many of us because we are drawn to speed and the spectacular. To be 'inefficient' doesn't mean we do things badly, nor does it mean we celebrate mediocrity, but it does invite us to reassess who we are and what we are capable of in life-giving and affirming ways. In the glare of social media platforms and the never-ending stream of 'success' news from colleagues and friends, our own frailty, vulnerability and 'inefficiency' may act as a form of grace rather than a hindrance to the work of God through us.

Walking: living in timefull ways

Naturally moving from slowness and 'inefficiency' we can explore living in ways that are more timefull. In the first few months of my job at Churches Together in England I was in conversation with a key ecumenical leader. He gave me some invaluable advice for the role. 'We have to learn to be better at wasting time with people,' he told me. While I wholeheartedly agreed with him it seemed that others found such a posture troubling, something to be suspicious of. National church leaders are busy people; if you want a meeting with them it must be purposeful, have a point, an agreed agenda ahead of time. What type of outcomes are anticipated for this meeting, I would be asked. 'I just want to waste some time with you' was, I found, not an answer greeted with much enthusiasm. There can be a feverishness about our time usage linked to an anxiety about our place in the world and in the work of God. If we truly believe that 'God became time with Christ', as Hauerwas reminds us it breaks the heavy, grasping nature of clock time in our lives. When we live in a way that embodies this model, we display a freedom from our self-importance, our anxiety about our place in the world; it means we are free to be for others.

In mission and ministry in the UK today we may reflect on the following questions:

1 How do we reveal that the biblical God is 'slow and ineffi-cient' in the midst of our busy UK lives – what does this mean for 'salvation today'?
2 What kind of ways of life will communicate salvation in the 'slow God' in the UK today?[9]
3 Do you embody the existential anxiety about the Church's place in the world? Or are you resisting the lure of speed and the spectacular?
4 How might we waste time with someone as an act of grace?

Seeing: practising 'neighbourology'

Koyama's experiences in Thailand convinced him that people would simply resist 'being objects of religious conquest' when they sensed there was only a one-way flow in traffic. Koyama says of his encounter with an elderly Thai woman in Chiang

Mai, 'I had a message for her, but I did not think that she had a message for me. She noticed this imperialistic one-sidedness.' 'Neighbourology' is about being truly encountering and being encountered by the other and the stranger. The stranger and the other can send us off course and confront us with our own parochialisms, self-obsessions and narrow-mindedness. Koyama maintained that in order for theology to be authentic it must be constantly challenged, disturbed and stirred up by the presence of strangers.[10]

The presence of strangers is becoming more of a reality in our daily lives. We live in an era when migration and the flow of peoples across the globe has reached an all-time high. The refugee agency UNHCR[11] suggests that there are over 83 million people who are currently forcibly displaced. The conflict in Syria, the Taliban regime in Afghanistan, the military Junta in Myanmar, and more recently the invasion of Ukraine, are some of the causes of the flow of people seeking safety and security. Others are moving for a better life or they are in mortal danger because of their sexual orientation or political affiliation. On top of these real and pressing concerns is the impact of climate change on the world's movement of the most vulnerable. More people will be on the move in the coming years as island nations are submerged and other areas become uninhabitable because of desertification. *How* we 'see' and *who* we 'see' is central to discipleship and mission. Whether we like it or not, migration and the movement of people across the globe will be a central part of the unfolding narrative for the UK's churches in the next decade and beyond. Are we able to extend hospitality to strangers? This is not to be some kind of disgruntled toleration of the stranger. We are not called to 'put up with' the other and avoid any real or meaningful contact but to divest ourselves of insularity and embrace the stranger. There are unhelpful traits in some of our Englishness that lean towards isolation and dismissiveness – these are not kingdom values. There are fantastic examples of communities taking Pope Francis's challenge that every parish, religious community, monastery in Europe take in a refugee family. Caritas in Salford[12] have been encouraging and equipping ordinary communities to help prepare a home, and welcome a refugee family, ensure that their children become settled in schools, and offer the means for the adults to learn English. To me, this seems a very good example of practising neighbourology. The recent kindness of many in opening their homes to Ukrainians fleeing the war is a wonderful thing and to be applauded.

But for Koyama it was more than welcoming and caring for the stranger in our midst. This was not to be a one-sided paternalistic process. We must be open to being changed by the stranger, being disrupted and challenged, to learn from them and be in a reciprocal relationship with them. Again, this is something we have found hard in the past. When the Windrush generation began to arrive in the UK in the 1950s and 1960s we failed both to welcome and learn from them. This cannot be allowed to happen again with the waves of migration now happening and which will continue to happen in the coming years. We need to see those who come to live among us as a gift – whether they are refugees, economic migrants or simply those who have left their homes because they are part of a growing number of men and women who feel called to re-evangelize the UK. Sometimes those gifts, as Rita shared in Chapter 3, can feel 'prickly' and that may well be a good thing.

Seeing: reflecting on our own 'bombing'

Koyama wrote that his encounter with black and Jewish people in New York had been like a 'second bombing' in his life. The history of oppression, persecution and appalling violence in the lives of these peoples made Koyama reassess his theology. Like his experience of wartime bombs raining down on Tokyo, it shaped his future theologizing. The death of George Floyd in May 2020 was a significant event that acted as a long over-due wake-up call for the Church in the UK around the issue of institutional racism and taking black experience seriously. All the historic denominations in the UK need to address these issues and make 'the table' at every gathering in the structures of church life bigger.

1 How do we take Koyama's assertion that Christian theology can only remain meaningful when it takes seriously the stranger?
2 Think about your own friendships. Who is at your table on a regular basis? Are there actions you can take to build intentional relationships across racial, socioeconomic and other divides?
3 What stories of oppression, systemic violence and persecution have been like 'bombing' experiences for you? How has it helped shape the way you do theology or think about God at work in the world?
4 What concrete actions can you take to ensure that refugees, asylum seekers and other immigrants find a welcome and a feeling of inclusion into UK life?

Talking: finding new metaphors to communicate grace

Lars Lindenberg reminds us that Koyama was very creative in his use of metaphor which he took from the surrounding culture. Koyama even drew his own illustrations in his book *50 Meditations*.[13] His ability to fuse unusual imagery and words is part of his brilliance as a theological teacher and communicator. The Christian Church has always been engaged in some form of translation work throughout its history. It has refashioned, appropriated, co-opted, bent and shaped words, images and metaphor in attempts to share the Jesus story; this has sometimes been done brilliantly – at other times it has been in dishearteningly shoddy ways.

Sometimes the Church can suffer from a poverty of metaphorical imagination. Perhaps we have too many tired metaphors – worn out, stumbling into cliché so that what we attempt to communicate is lost or laughable. Archbishop Stephen Cottrell at the Estates Evangelism Task Group in November 2021 recalled how he led an Anglo Catholic mission to a parish in Middlesbrough in the 1990s. At the end of each day a group of priests, nuns and monks would gather in the pub opposite the church. By the Saturday they had gained minor celebrity status, so unusual was their presence. In the bar that evening there was a karaoke machine in one corner and a DJ in the other. After taking the mic, the archbishop gave a rousing rendition of Gloria Gaynor's 'I will survive'. At the end of this, the DJ in the other corner of the room shouted across: 'Why do you sing songs that nobody knows?'

The archbishop said, 'I found myself kind of making almost a public apology to the people of that estate who had been disenfranchised by their own church, that somehow our church culture had got so removed from their lives that there was no longer any connection.' Archbishop Stephen's story exposes a gap. But it is not only a gap – it is at times a poverty of imagination and an unwillingness to contextualize, and an attitude towards a culture we live at odds with. Bevan's models of doing contextual theology that I referred to in Chapter 1 remind us that while we might naturally start from different ends of the spectrum depending on our theology, denomination or life experience, we can find fruit in acknowledging them without being trapped by them.

We need to craft new metaphors to communicate the stories of grace that weave themselves through the New Testament and on into the lives of the saints past and present. In twenty-first-century mission we need to embrace the creative, becoming poets, painters and pencillers of prose. Hammering out more malleable metaphors that speak to the sonorities of people's lives, loves, losses and longings. Archbishop Stephen has called on the Church to be shaped by the refining fire of questions, and the recent announcement of the new Centre for Cultural Witness may be an important part of the process.[14]

Talking: leaning into postures of 'listening' and 'the apophatic' for evangelism

Koyama writes that for 400 years the Church in Asia was all but useless at listening to the voices and experiences of indigenous peoples. Almost everywhere, the church has been – and in many cases continues to be – deaf. Koyama was deeply concerned not only at the lack of listening, but the talking that the Church has done. Much of the talk has been one way. Telling. Talking without listening. Monological missiology. For those of us at the sharp end of evangelism and mission, these accusations are painful and poignant. Perhaps we have been drawn into the noisy competitive nature of the world. The Church has sometimes employed the 'get a bigger microphone' policy in its attempts to engage the world with the story of Jesus for fear of being drowned out by a cacophony of other voices. Stephen Hance's recent research on how the general public perceive the Church of England was a painful reminder that 'very many people have no particular sense or feeling about the Church one way or the other ... Most people don't think about us at all.'[15] We are approached with benign indifference, and this reality is difficult for many of us to swallow. In a world bad at listening and in a political landscape of increasing polarization where shouting down one's opponent is the norm how do we recover an evangelism rooted in listening?

In Chapter 4 I wasn't trying to suggest that evangelism is entirely about listening but making the point that we need to redress the balance and put forward the idea that words are not always the primary evidence. Our logocentric world needs to be tempered. What if we believed more in the potential power of art or poetry as a vessel for evangelism? Do we really believe that those with limited 'voice' have a significant role to play in *missio Dei*? How often have we treated people as our evangelistic projects, and in a small way diminished them without intending to do so? Are we able to develop notions of evangelism that are based in silence, stillness, soul accompaniment, sharing bread together, sitting with unanswered questions? In the light of the past few years and our global vulnerabilities, we may need to learn to do so more readily.

1 Do you sense the Church has done too much talking? How do we find a balance between listening and speaking in our evangelistic endeavours?
2 Who might we have excluded from the joy of sharing the gospel because we have been too logocentric in our evangelism? What steps can we take to redress the balance?
3 What 'tired' metaphors should we discard because they are worn and hinder us rather than help?
4 Might you find mileage in the idea of 'anamchara' for walking with people towards Jesus?

Surrendering: on being 'inefficient' and immobile

In Chapter 5 on surrendering we thought about the way in which the Church has struggled to relinquish temporal power and wanting to side with the powerful and well resourced. Koyama says that 'Jesus abandons himself to human dominance, even to crucifixion. This inefficient way is the secret of his power that confronts human power. It is the secret of his love.' I suggested that we have much to learn from the gift of those who may be slow cognitively or in terms of mobility. Rather than being a defeatist posture, surrendering to our own limitations and vulnerabilities is in fact the secret to joining in with God's mission to the world. Some of the most potent theological reflections in the history of the Church have been forged in places (physical, mental and emotional) of limitation and darkness. We need the experiences of the whole Church in all its chaotic gloriousness to share the whole gospel with the whole world.

Koyama was also concerned about the power that technology possessed to create illusion or *maya* us. He felt too often human beings could be tempted by the feelings of efficiency, speed and power that technology creates. In this, Koyama felt that 'efficiency collapses meaning' and we end up being dehumanized by technology. I tried to argue that technology in its many forms offers hope for the future, but the darker side of technology's seeming salvation from limitation, fragility and powerlessness must be resisted. The promises of transhumanism, for example, have seriously dystopian elements that we need to assess and not be naive about.

The exponential rise in the use of the digital in our church life during the pandemic threw up a number of questions and problems. While some saw it as an unprecedented missional opportunity, others were more sceptical about the future. The great democratization around access to online worship took place, but it was also offset by some denominations restricting access to the Eucharist for theological reasons – and in some cases practical ones. The worrisome issue of social media and the way in which we engage others in conversation and debate continues to mirror the fractious relationships in a polarized world. #Anglican Twitter seems to be on the edge of implosion most days, and yet there are stories and individuals who counter the venom and curmudgeonly attitudes of some users. The death of Sister Catherine Wybourne, whose twitter handle was @digitalnun, in late February 2022 brought an outpouring of grief by those who acknowledged her as 'a generous, holy, kind, and humorous presence on Twitter'.[16] Clearly, there are ways to 'be' in digital spheres that reflect the mercy, grace, complexity and joy of being a follower of Jesus. Unfortunately, it can feel unbalanced at times.

Surrendering: the joy of divine irrelevance

Lastly, I suggested that we needed to be more in touch with our dust and ashes identity. Koyama felt that in the story of Abraham in Genesis 18 he had uncovered an important 'living in the face of death' amid life. This self-identity as dust and ashes provided Abraham with spiritual, psychological and intellectual energy to wrestle with problems.

Such is our desire for significance that surrendering to our own frail bodies and our own mortality is difficult; sometimes impossible. In the act of surrendering, we learn more deeply that 'discipleship is quite simply the extended training in being dispossessed. Unless we learn to relinquish our presumption that we can ensure the significance of our lives, we are not capable of the peace of the kingdom.'[17] Søren Kierkegaard, the nineteenth-century Danish philosopher, said, 'What the age needs is not a genius but a martyr.' Too often we have thought the world was in need of clever answers rather than broken people.

Living with a close acknowledgement of our own mortality, our death amid life, our frailties, vulnerabilities and limitations makes us secure in the one beyond death and less concerned with our own egos. We can be for others. I think this is a profoundly attractive way to live for emerging generations. I was struck by two Zoom calls I happened to take part in one afternoon towards the end of writing this book. Both gathered under-thirties in significant conversations around ecumenism and church planting. Again and again, the participants used phrases relating to authenticity, vulnerability, inclusivity and sustainability to talk about faith and engagement with the world. I came out of the meetings feeling incredibly hopeful that at least a generation of younger people on the cusp of filling significant leadership roles 'get it'. In the light of surrender we might ask:

1 How do we live well in digital spaces and social media platforms as our authentic selves?
2 How do we live in the light that we are 'dust and ashes' without becoming fatalistic or disillusioned?
3 How do we live out our 'divine irrelevance' in the world when we are often told the Church needs to be culturally relevant?
4 How do we as Christians, as 'beings inseparable from death', reveal a way of living that doesn't push death to the edge of our existence?

Closing words

It seems to me that Koyama is a prophetic voice for us as Christians living in the early part of the twenty-first century. His writing urges us not to be taken in or consumed by modernism's obsessions with speed, power, efficiency, status and prestige, but instead to be captured by a vision of Jesus – the one who became 'inefficient' for us. The incarnate one shows us how to live with weakness and limitation as gift rather than as deficiency. Christ became time for us that we, when living faithfully, have all the time in the world to join God in his mission.

I have found that my most helpful readings of Koyama have been when I treated him like the sage and spiritual director I believe him to be. I have read him in digestible daily 'tasting plates', nourishing my soul when I felt overwhelmed by the pressure to do something spectacular when all I could muster was a slow plod in the right direction. May you also be nourished and encouraged as you read him too.

Notes

1 K. Koyama, 1968, 'Christian Presence in the Light of Our Theme: In Him All Things Hold Together', *The South East Asian Journal of Theology* 10(1), p. 13.

2 L. Newbigin, 1985, *Unfinished Agenda: An Autobiography*, Grand Rapids, MI: Eerdmans, p. 254.

3 Newbigin, *Unfinished Agenda*, p. 15.

4 Newbigin, *Unfinished Agenda*, p. 16.

5 Newbigin, *Unfinished Agenda*, p. 17.

6 K. Koyama, 1982, 'Christ at the Periphery', *The Ecumenical Review* 34(1), p. 68.

7 K. Koyama, 1974, *Waterbuffalo Theology*, London: SCM Press, p. 4.

8 Luke 2.24 and Leviticus 12.8.

9 Koyama, *Waterbuffalo Theology*, p. 5.

10 K. Koyama, 1993, '"Extend Hospitality to Strangers" – A Missiology of Theologia Crucis', *International Review of Mission* 82(327), p. 283.

11 UNHCR, 'Figures at a Glance', *UNHCR UK*, https://www.unhcr. org/uk/figures-at-a-glance.html, accessed 5.4.2022.

12 Diocese of Salford, 'Community Sponsorship of Refugees', *Caritas Diocese of Salford*, https://www.caritassalford.org.uk/service-view/ community-sponsorship-of-refugees/, accessed 5.4.2022.

13 L. Lindberg, 1996, 'Koyama, the Cross and Sweden in Dialogue' in D. Irvin and A. Akinade (eds), *The Agitated Mind of God: The Theology of Kosuke Koyama*, Maryknoll, NY: Orbis Books, p. 99.

14 M. Davies, 2022, 'Lambeth to house new unit to explain and promote Christian faith', *Church Times*, 16 February, https://www. churchtimes.co.uk/articles/2022/18-february/news/uk/lambeth-to-house-new-unit-to-explain-and-promote-christian-faith, accessed 5.4.2022.

15 M. Davies, 2021, 'Public does not think much of C of E, the Revd Dr Stephen Hance reports', *Church Times*, 12 November, https://www. churchtimes.co.uk/articles/2021/12-november/news/uk/public-does-not-think-much-of-c-of-e-the-revd-dr-stephen-hance-reports, accessed 5.4.2022.

16 Dr Jo Kershaw (@mrth_jo), 2022, *Twitter*, 24 February, https:// twitter.com/mthr_jo/status/1496954975565586433, accessed 5.4.2022.

17 S. Hauerwas, 1983, *The Peaceable Kingdom: A Primer in Christian Ethics*, Notre Dame, IN: University of Notre Dame Press, p. 86.

Bibliography

Baudrillard, J., 1994, *Simulacra and Simulation*, Ann Arbor, MI: University of Michigan Press.

Begbie, J., 2000, *Theology, Music and Time*, Cambridge: Cambridge University Press.

Bevans, S. B., 1985, 'Models of Contextual Theology', *Missiology: An International Review* 13(2), pp. 185–202.

Bevans, S. B., 2002, *Models of Contextual Theology*, Maryknoll, NY: Orbis Books.

Bevans, S. B. and R. Schroeder, 2011, *Prophetic Dialogue on Christian Mission Today*, Maryknoll, NY: Orbis Books.

Bevans, S. B. and K. Tahaafe-Williams (eds), 2011, *Contextual Theology for the Twenty-First Century*, Eugene, OR: Pickwick Publications.

Bonhoeffer, D., 1997, *Letters and Papers from Prison*, ed. Eberhard Bethge, New York: Touchstone.

Bosch, D., 1980, *Witness to the World: The Christian Mission in Theological Perspective*, Eugene, OR: Wipf & Stock.

Bosch, D., 1981, 'In Search of Mission: Reflections on "Melbourne" and "Pattaya"', *Missionalia* 9(1).

Bosch, D., 1988, '"Ecumenicals" and "Evangelicals": A Growing Relationship?', *The Ecumenical Review* 40(3–4), p. 472.

Bosch, D., 1991, *Transforming Mission: Paradigm Shifts in Theology of Mission*, Maryknoll, NY: Orbis Books.

Bria, I., 1993, 'Dynamics of Mission in Liturgy', *International Review of Mission* 82(327).

Chow, A. and J. Kurlberg, 2020, 'Two or Three Gathered Online: Asian and European Responses to COVID 19 and the Digital Church', *Studies in World Christianity* 26(3).

Chow, A. and E. Wild-Wood (eds), 2020, *Ecumenism and Independency in World Christianity: Historical Studies in Honour of Brian Stanley*, Leiden: Brill.

Cruchley-Jones, P., 2016, 'Evangelism from the Margins: Experiences of the Ironic in Evangelism in Cardiff, UK', *International Review of Mission* 105(1).

Dorling, D. and S. Tomlinson, 2019, *Rule Britannia: Brexit and the End of Empire*, London: Biteback Publishing.

Fuimara, G. C., 1990, *The Other Side of Language: A Philosophy of Listening*, Oxford: Routledge.

Graham, E., 2009, *Word Made Flesh: Writings in Pastoral and Practical Theology*, London: SCM Press.

Gros, F., 2015, *A Philosophy of Walking*, London: Verso.

Hauerwas, S., 1983, *The Peaceable Kingdom: A Primer in Christian Ethics*, Notre Dame, IN: University of Notre Dame Press.

Heath, E. A., 2008, *The Mystic Way of Evangelism: A Contemplative Vision for Christian Outreach*, Grand Rapids, MI: Baker Academic.

Herman, A. and C. Burlacioiu, 2016, 'Current Debates About the Approach of the "Munich School" and Further Perspectives on the Interdisciplinary Study of the History of World Christianity', *Journal of World Christianity* 6(1).

Hiebert, P., 1994, *Anthropological Reflections on Missiological Issues*, Grand Rapids, MI: Baker Books.

Hollinghurst, S., 2010, *Mission Shaped Evangelism: The Gospel in Contemporary Society*, Norwich: Canterbury Press.

Honoré, C., 2004, *In Praise of Slow*, London: Orion Publishing.

Hunt, H. A., 2011, 'The History of the Lausanne Movement, 1974–1989', *International Review of Missionary Research* 35(2).

Irvin, D., 2013, 'The Ritual of the Limping Dance: Kosuke Koyama's Positive Assessment of Pluralism for Christian Theology', *Journal of Ecumenical Studies* 48(3).

Irvin, D. and A. Akinade (eds), 1996, *The Agitated Mind of God: The Theology of Kosuke Koyama*, Maryknoll, NY: Orbis Books.

Jackelén, A., 2019, 'The Need for a Theology of Resilience, Coexistence and Hope', *The Ecumenical Review* 70(1–2).

Jantzen, G., 1983, 'Time and Timelessness' in A. Richardson and J. Bowden (eds), *A New Dictionary of Christian Theology*, London: SCM Press.

Johnson, S., 2015, *How We Got to Now: Six Innovations That Made the Modern World*, London: Penguin.

Keith, B., 2017, 'Exploring Attitudes to Evangelism: An Ethnographic Study of Street Angels and Club Angels', *Anvil* 33(2).

Kelsey, D., 2009, *Eccentric Existence: A Theological Anthropology* (2 vols), St Louisville, KY: Westminster John Knox Press.

Kirk, A., 1999, *What Is Mission? Theological Explorations*, London: Darton, Longman & Todd.

Kool, M. A., 2016, 'A Missiologist's look at the Future: A Missiological Manifesto for the 21st Century' in C. Constantineanu, M. V. Măcelaru, A. M. Kool and M. Himcinschi (eds), *Mission in Central and Eastern Europe: Realities, Perspectives, Trends*, Oxford: Regnum.

Koyama, K., 1968, 'Christian Presence in the Light of Our Theme: In Him All Things Hold Together', *South East Asian Journal of Theology* 10(1).

Koyama, K., 1974, *Waterbuffalo Theology*, London: SCM Press.

Koyama, K., 1975, '"Not by Bread Alone..." How Does Jesus Free Us and Unite Us?', *Ecumenical Review* 24(3).

Koyama, K., 1977, *No Handle on the Cross: An Asian Meditation on the Crucified Mind*, London: SCM Press.

Koyama, K., 1979, *50 Meditations*, Maryknoll, NY: Orbis Books.

Koyama, K., 1979, *Three Mile an Hour God*, London: SCM Press.

Koyama, K., 1980, 'The Crucified Christ Challenges Human Power' in *Your Kingdom Come: Mission Perspectives – Report on the World Conference of Mission and Evangelism*, Geneva: World Council of Churches.

Koyama, K., 1982, 'Christ at the Periphery', *Ecumenical Review* 34(1).

Koyama, K., 1984, *Mount Fuji and Mount Sinai*, London: SCM Press.

Koyama, K., 1993, '"Extend Hospitality to Strangers" – A Missiology of Theologia Crucis', *International Review of Mission* 82(327).

Koyama, K., 1997, 'My Pilgrimage in Mission', *International Bulletin of Missionary Research* 21(2).

Koyama, K., 2003, 'Reformation in the Global Context: The Disturbing Spaciousness of Jesus Christ', *Currents in Theology and Mission* 30(2).

Kwiyani, H., 2019, 'Can the West Really be Converted?', *Missio Africanus Journal of African Missiology* 4(1).

Kwiyani, H., 2020, 'Mission After George Floyd: On White Supremacy, Colonialism and World Christianity', *Anvil* 36(3).

Mase, H., 1985, 'Death and Dying: Towards an Ethic of Death', *Currents in Theology and Mission* 12(2).

Morse, M., 1991, *Kosuke Koyama: A Model for Intercultural Theology*, Frankfurt am Main: Peter Lang.

Mosebach, M., 2019, *The 21: A Journey into the Land of the Coptic Martyrs*, Robertsbridge: Plough Publishing House.

Moynagh, M., 2012, *A Church in Every Context: An Introduction to Theology and Practice*, London: SCM Press.

Newbigin, L., 1979, 'Not Whole without the Handicapped' in G. Müller-Fahrenholz (ed.), *Partners in Life: The Handicapped and the Church*, Geneva: World Council of Churches.

Newbigin, L., 1985, *Unfinished Agenda: An Autobiography*, Grand Rapids, MI: Eerdmans.

Newbigin, L., 1986, *Foolishness to the Greeks*, London: SPCK.

Nouwen, H., 1989, *In the Name of Jesus: Reflections on Christian Leadership*, New York: Crossroad.

Novsima, I., 2019, 'A Nonverbal Mission: An Apophatic Missiology from the Trauma Experience of Women with Intellectual Disabilities in Indonesia', *International Review of Mission* 108(1).

O'Donnell, K., 2018, 'Performing the Imago Dei: Human Enhancement, Artificial Intelligence and Operative Image Bearing', *International Journal for the Study of the Christian Church* 18(1).

O'Donnell, K., 2021, 'The Theologian as Dreamer: On Theological Imagination and Human Enhancement', *Theology* 124(5).

Olofinjana, I., 2021, *Discipleship, Suffering and Racial Justice: Mission in a Pandemic World*, Oxford: Regnum.

Paas, S., 2019, *Pilgrims and Priests: Christian Mission in a Post-Christian Society*, London: SCM Press.

Paas, S., 2021, 'Missional Christian Communities in Conditions of Marginality: On Finding a "Missional Existence" in the Post-Christian West', *Mission Studies* 38(1).

Pachuau, L., 2018, *World Christianity: A Historical and Theological Introduction*, Nashville, TN: Abingdon Press.

Pope Francis, 2013, *Evangelii gaudium*, Vatican: Libreria Editrice Vaticana.

Reddie, A., 2018, 'Now You See Me, Now You Don't: Subjectivity, Blackness, and Difference in Practical Theology in Britain post Brexit', *Practical Theology* 11(1).

Ritzer, J., 1998, *The McDonaldization Thesis*, London: Sage.

Rohr, R., 2012, *Falling Upwards*, London: SPCK.

Rollins, P., 2006, *How (Not) to Speak of God*, London: SPCK Press.

Romus, J., 2001, 'Evangelization in the Contemporary Roman Catholic Thought', *Indian Journal of Theology* 43(1 & 2).

Ross, K., J. Keum, K. Avtzi and R. Hewitt (eds), 2016, *Ecumenical Missiology: Changing Landscapes and New Conceptions of Mission*, Oxford: Regnum.

Schwab, K., 2016, *The Fourth Industrial Revolution*, London: Penguin Random House.

Solnit, R., 2002, *Wanderlust: A History of Walking*, London: Granta.

Stanislaus, L. and C. Tauchner (eds), 2020, *Becoming Intercultural: Perspectives on Mission*, New Delhi: iSPCK.

Swinton, J., 2010, 'Who Is the God We Worship? Theologies of Disability; Challenges and New Possibilities', *International Journal of Practical Theology* 14(1).

Swinton, J., 2017, *Becoming Friends of Time: Disability, Timefullness, and Gentle Discipleship*, London: SCM Press.

Thang, D. M., 2017, 'The Crucified Mind: Kosuke Koyama's Missiology of "Theology of the Cross"', *Exchange* 43(1).

Villa-Vicencio, C. (ed), 1988, *Theology and Violence: The South African Debate*, Grand Rapids, MI: Eerdmans.

Walls, F. A., 2014, 'Mission and Migration: The Diaspora Factor in Christian History' in C. H. Im and A. Yong (eds), *Global Diasporas and Mission*, Oxford: Regnum.

Warren, R., 1996, *Signs of Life: How Goes the Decade of Evangelism?*, London: Church House Publishing.

Welby, J., 2018, *Reimagining Britain: Foundations for Hope*, London: Bloomsbury Continuum.

Williams, R., 2003, *Silence and Honey Cakes: The Wisdom of the Desert*, London: Lion Books.

Index of Names and Subjects

50 Meditations (Koyama) 8, 162

Augustine of Canterbury 40–1
anxiety 2, 25, 34, 49, 56, 71,
    76–7, 82, 152, 159

Baudrillard, Jean 136–7
Begbie, Jeremy 38–40
Benedict, St 41
Bevans, Stephen 9–12
    Models of Contextual Theology
    10–11
Black Lives Matter (BLM) 71
Bonhoeffer, Dietrich 110, 127
Bosch, David 21, 23, 24, 69, 102
Brexit 79, 80, 81, 82
Bushido 17, 19–20

Cambodia 3, 6–7, 15, 32–3,
    115–18
Christendom 116, 117, 121
Christianity 13, 74, 82, 87, 96–7,
    105, 127, 142
    in Japan 17–18, 28n35
    religionless 110
    Western 83, 104, 106
    world 20–1, 23–5, 75, 82
Christian Enquiry Agency 147
Church of England 47–9, 50, 54,
    57, 164
church growth 24, 48, 51, 53, 57,
    70, 146
Churches Together in England
    (CTE) 5, 100, 158

Church Mission Society (CMS)
    22, 73
Community Supper 58
contextual theology 7, 9–11, 105,
    163
coronavirus, Covid pandemic 45,
    50, 71, 78, 82, 100, 128–9,
    143, 149, 151

death 19, 39, 103, 126, 127–9,
    149–52, 167
digital 134–5, 136–8, 146, 167
    Centre for Digital Theology 140
    Charter 147
    church 26, 48, 142–7
    engagement 128, 166
    poverty 145
disability 110–12, 127, 131–3

ecumenism, ecumenical
    movement 8–9, 20–1, 23–4, 83,
    156–7, 167
Eiesland, Nancy 132, 152n5
empire 9, 67, 75–9, 81, 103, 108,
    113, 117
European Christian Mission
    (ECM) 82
evangelism
    as listening 105–8
    apophatic 109–10
    Catholic understanding of 102
    Group for 106
    Orthodox understanding of
    102–3

'spat upon' 115–17
'stigma of Jesus' 113–14
exceptionalism 78, 79, 80

feast 72
Fiumara, Gemma Corradi 105
food 1, 15, 72–3, 83
Fresh Expressions of church 46, 48, 59, 105

General Synod 47, 81

Holy Trinity Brompton 52–3
Hauerwas, Stanley 56, 152n5, 159
hospitality 25, 65–7, 70–1, 82, 87, 91, 121, 160

idolatry 17, 31, 79, 98, 126, 127, 133–4, 155
Imago Dei 70, 107, 108, 122, 140
imperialism 8, 18, 73, 74, 79
industrial revolution 2, 38, 137
intercultural church 87–90
inefficiency 18, 49, 97, 129, 131, 149, 155, 157

Jackelén, Antje 77–80
Japan 7–9, 13–20, 68, 133, 134, 151

Khmer Rouge 32–3
Kwiyani, Harvey 75–6, 85, 101

Lausanne movement 22–4
listening 54–5, 69, 75, 97–8
logocentric 105, 110, 164–5

Makgoba, Thabo 67
manifest destiny 79
margins, marginalized 10, 19, 55, 65–7, 75, 80, 98, 103, 104, 110–11, 115–16, 157

maya 135
measuring 50, 57, 59
Mingei movement 14, 20
migration 25, 67, 71, 80–1, 87–8, 91, 160–1
Missio Dei 21, 22, 46, 56, 70, 107, 111, 118, 122, 133
missiology 9, 50, 71, 86, 87, 91, 97, 164
mission 6, 8, 21–5, 33, 45–6, 51–2, 56, 66–8, 69, 70, 73–6, 85–6, 96–8, 100, 102, 104, 108, 110–13, 117–18, 127–8, 131–3, 146, 148, 158–60, 163, 164, 165–6
missionaries 18, 75, 82–3, 86, 105, 114
Mount Fuji and Mount Sinai (Koyama) 133
Moynagh, Mike 52, 55, 108

neighbourhood 46, 60, 88, 130
neighbourology 67–70, 159–61
Newbigin, Lesslie 57, 133, 156
No Handle on the Cross 8
Novsima, Isabella 110, 111, 113

OMF Internationl 117–18

Paas, Stefan 98, 100, 104, 111, 116
pan-Christian 24, 155
Partnership for Missional Church (PMC) 108
patriarchy 77, 80
periphery 9, 65, 97, 98, 115, 155–7
pilgrimage 59, 68, 98, 133
A Pilgrim's Progress (John Bunyan) 8
pioneer minister 49, 50, 54, 55, 107
polarization 77–8, 164
populism 77–9

postcolonial 23, 77, 86
post-truth 77, 80
protectionism

resource church 'model' 45, 48,
    51–5
Roxburgh, Alan 47

sawubona 67
serving 82, 114
'serving-first' model 55
slowness 8, 25, 35, 43–5, 98,
    105, 120, 121, 122, 127, 157,
    158
South Africa 4–5, 15, 58, 66, 72,
    75, 77, 89–90, 146, 149, 150
  Group Areas Act 4
speed 15, 16, 20, 31, 33, 36,
    38–9, 42–5, 49, 51, 105, 131,
    155, 158–9, 165, 168
stranger 67, 70–1, 73, 85, 87, 91,
    160–2
Strategic Development Fund
    (SDF) 46–52
Strategic Development Unit
    (SDU) 49–50
subjugation 74, 76, 79, 117
Swinton, John 36, 40, 41, 56,
    112, 131–2, 142, 152n5

technicity 136
technology 15–16, 44, 47, 81,
    128, 133–9, 147–9, 165–6
theology 6–10, 16–17, 31, 45,
    69, 74–5, 95–7, 105, 132, 133,
    155, 160, 163
  African 86

Christian 70, 85, 109, 127, 162
disability 127, 131–2
of evangelism 96
in Japan 16–18, 28n35
of mission 21, 102
minority 85
Orthodox 139
'Three Mile an Hour God' 31,
    59–60, 117, 129
Three Mile An Hour God
    (Koyama) 8, 17
time
  chronos 42–4
  clock 36–9, 41
  God 39
  kairos 42–4
timefull, timefullness 1, 30, 31,
    39, 42, 49
Tokyo 7, 15, 31, 43, 66, 126, 161

violence 25, 42, 67, 68, 73–6, 91,
    108, 161
Virilio, Paul 42

walking 30–5, 158
Walls, Andrew 81
World Conference on Mission and
    Evangelism 5, 23
World Council of Churches
    (WCC) 20–4, 110, 114
World War Two 8, 14, 20, 43,
    79, 126, 134
worship 19, 26, 41, 42, 71, 90,
    143, 144, 166
'worship-first' model 52, 55

Xavier, Francis 17